Resilience In The Storm

By Tricia Andreassen

Co-Authored by:
Jordan Andreassen
Chris Blackburn
Dawn Briggs
Janet DiTroia
Betsy Ferguson
Dave Frett
Gary King
Cindy Lea
Coni K. Meyers
Karen White
Mark Williams

Creative Life Publishing & Learning Institute
www.CLPLI.com
Info@CLPLI.com

Book Versions
Paperback ISBN: 978-1-946265-00-5
Hardback ISBN: 978-1-946265-03-6
eBook ISBN: 978-1-946265-01-2
Amazon ISBN: 978-1-946265-02-9

Cover Design By Dara Rogers

Copyright © 2016
Creative Life Publishing & Learning Institute

REALTOR® and NAR are registered trademarks.

All rights reserved. No part of this book may be reproduced in any form without prior written permission from the publisher. This work represents the views and opinions of the author alone. No liability in conjunction with the content or the use of ideas connected with this work is assumed by the publisher.

THE HOLY BIBLE, NEW INTERNATIONAL VERSION®, NIV® Copyright © 1973, 1978, 1984, 2011 by Biblica, Inc.® Used by permission. All rights reserved worldwide.

"New International Version" and "NIV" are registered trademarks of Biblica, Inc.®.

Contents

Dedication | 5

Resilience In The Storm by Tricia Andreassen | 7

"Life" In The Ring by Chris Blackburn | 41

Looking In The Mirror by Janet DiTroia | 59

Suicide Is Never The Answer by Jordan Andreassen | 71

Giving It To God by Cindy Lea | 81

Taking On Water by Dave Frett | 95

The Identity Of Resilience by Dawn Briggs | 109

The Fuel Of A Purposed Life by Coni Meyers | 121

Again Spring by Mark Williams | 135

God Might Wreck Your Dreams by Betsy Ferguson | 151

Living Like Drew by Karen White | 163

Life Is A Journey of Retakes by Gary King | 177

Layers Of LIFE by Tricia Andreassen | 185

The Reflection Of Resilience by Tricia Andreassen | 197

After The Storm – Finding Your Way Back | 201
by Tricia Andreassen

Dedication

This book is dedicated to my Heavenly Father above and to all of the Authors who willing shared their personal stories of triumph. I also want to dedicate this book to my Pastor, Steven Furtick. I truly feel that God led me to his leadership and as he poured into me, the message of resilience was born. I am forever grateful for my loving and supportive husband who has the quiet strength of resilience and is the love of my life. I am also so proud of my son Jordan stepping out in sharing his message as a youth leader.

- Tricia Andreassen

RESILIENCE IN THE STORM
by Tricia Andreassen

RESILIENCE IN THE STORM

"Storms make trees take deeper roots." – Dolly Parton

Have you ever watched intensely the movement of a tree when a storm is upon it? With the wind and the rain, it somehow stays rooted in its foundation underneath. Leaves may blow off some of the branches. Some of the branches may fall away and still the heart of the tree stays strong in the face of some of the most incredible seasons that could cause it to die. Yet, somehow, the tree stands. Sure, it may experience some damage. It may look like it has taken a beating. Then as the weather changes into the bright glow of the sun above, and the peace of the wind rustles through the leaves, it blossoms from that storm. The rain that came was divinely prepared to take that rainwater and nourish the heart of that tree so that it would thrive. Blossoms emerged from the combination of that rain and the rays of the sun; casting down its nutrients so it could be better than what it was from before.

That is what comes to my mind, spirit, and soul when I think of resilience. It is standing in the storm. It is having the faith and hope that you will not only rebound but you will come out stronger than before.

Perhaps that is what I was thinking the week of Christmas 2015 when I was up at my 4:30am writing time. I was at my husband's family home in Michigan. The only one up in the house, drinking my coffee with my candles lit beside me, a feeling of contemplation came over me. I was reflecting on what the last year and a half had been like. It was sincerely some of the worst times since I had experienced a miscarriage and divorce in 1997. I was thinking in this moment, *"I have come through the other side…I have weathered through the worst, and I am still standing strong."*

And in that moment I did feel that. I had the sense of optimism and of hope for this next chapter of my life. I had sold my company that I had worked a third of my life to build and would give me financial freedom. I had prepared…I had chosen a company that I believed was reputable based off of perceptions of others. Did I have an intuition that maybe the transaction shouldn't be trusted? Yes. But, I pushed it off my mind in hopes that my sixth sense was off. I was so ready for this new chapter of my life to do what I felt God had called me to do that I took things into my own hands on who I decided to sell to; even though my intuition was telling me something.

My evolved sense of intuition has always been strong.

Leadership expert John Maxwell commented in a teaching session one day. He said, *"Prayer is when you talk to God. And intuition is when God is talking to you."* That caused me to commit to memory and write that down. And yet, I have been guilty of not listening to what God may be saying at the time. I have met people in a moment and have been able to know the truth. It is in those moments he doesn't leave me. He teaches me. He guides me. He provides me resilience. Through these moments I have gained incredible insight that now has taught me to truly walk in the direction of where God is ordering my steps. I lay every relationship, opportunity and even business client on the altar, taking it to him first. If it were not for the lessons that are provided in moments of challenge I would not have that wisdom today. It is something that is so priceless I wouldn't change it for a thing.

Let's go back to that morning of when the intuition of the word 'resilience' came to me. It was the little voice inside me that said, *"Tricia, you need to gather people together to share their story on the topic of resilience."* The thought inspired me; hungry to learn more about how to build resilience. In my mind, I also rationalized to myself, "*Just look at you, Tricia. Look at all the things you have gone through and now it's time to share your story of resilience.*" Little did I know that I had no idea the level of resilience I would learn in comparison to what was to come over the next six months. It would prove that resilience is not a 'one-time' thing. It is an ever-growing, ever-evolving process of growth and awareness.

Up until right now, at this moment my fingers are hitting the keyboard, I wasn't going to share the intimate struggles that faced me over the last two years or even touch on the last several months no less. It was only until I began reading the chapters of these incredible people in this book. The talks with them gave me the courage to share more about my most recent journey and sincerely share the walk I am in at this exact moment. I personally have come to understand that one of the key principles in holding on during a storm of adversity is having those in your life that can be there to lift you up in the right time.

Why do I say that? It was in this project of resilience that God had called me to bring these people together, to share their stories so they could LIFT ME UP in this particular life chapter.

It brings reflection back to that early morning and the conversation with dear friend Vickie Smith. I shared with her my thought on a book that featured stories of resilience. Her response was, "*I love it. Resilience, is not talked about often enough and it is what keeps us going.*"

From then on, things started to gain momentum. The next week my second cousin Elizabeth came to my mind. We had only seen each other once in about 27 years (I know, right!) but the gift of Social Media had brought us back together in connection. One night a few months prior she had messaged me and said

"Hey cousin, I have this feeling that God wants me to write a book." I didn't know what her topic was at the time, but I shared with her my thoughts on how to get started. Life continued on until she came to my mind about this book. She was excited and said she would love to be a part of it. It was only about a month or two later she told me, *"Tricia, did you know that when I was just eleven years old, God told me I was going to write a book on resilience? The day you called me I literally had to pull my car over to the side of the road because it just about knocked the wind out of me!"*

It was the first confirmation of God's hand on this work.

To use the analogy of weather, the outlook seemed sunny. I was truly enjoying researching about resilience and talking to many others about their experiences. In those conversations, I ended up connecting with a childhood friend who knew me from about five years old. Again we had not seen each other in over 23 years, but social media had connected us. In a conversation, I mentioned to him the book I felt God had called me to put together. Chris Blackburn and I talked on the phone and in that moment we knew we were to collaborate on this message. His life journey had taken him through different paths, and he was dedicated to sharing his message to help others. Again, his heart and spirit touched me beyond measure.

Calls with others like Janet DiTroia that was a client from years ago reconnected out of the blue sharing her message of healing and loving yourself. Her message was incredibly inspiring. Dawn Briggs who I never met physically in person and only through mutual connections on Facebook became friends with me. We ended up talking for hours. We prayed in the spirit, and God took over in what was going to be delivered in the word. Even in that moment of the conversation I remember Dawn being very ill and fighting through the spiritual warfare. The negative voice in her head kept saying to her, *"Why bother being in this book, you are so sick you won't be alive to see it anyway."* Thank God we fought that voice side by side. The enemy was attacking hard to stop this message she was to share. I prayed right then over the phone, and the prophetic message came out that she was meant to help others walk through this uncertainty of physical ailments as well as other emotional afflictions.

My faithful friend and Author Coni Meyers joined into the project to share her personal insights as well as the beautiful leader (and mom of a young one), Betsy Ferguson. Her story was meant to be told. In all sincerity, resilience could be Betsy's middle name, and you will read more about that as well. If it weren't for Betsy reading my business book on marketing and then attending my women's life retreat, we would have never bonded to the level we did. Dave Frett was introduced to me through Betsy as he had a calling to write a devotional book. I wasn't going to bring up the resilience project since the other book was his focus but God wouldn't allow me to stop thinking about him. In the middle of the night, I was told, *"Dave is supposed to be in this project."* So, I listened, and I shared the heart behind it. Another connection from my past, Cindy Lea a high school classmate who I also hadn't seen in decades emerged saying she felt that she was to share her message of resilience. A police officer for over 20 years and a wonderful example of a servant's heart, I was honored by who was coming into the vision for this project. In interviewing Gary King, Author of *"The Happiness Formula"* my heart was so touched by his wisdom that he also graciously contributed to this book. Through these unique connections, I knew this would be a MOVEMENT, not just a book.

As a coach and speaker for John Maxwell on leadership, I had built relationships with other like-minded teachers in daily calls and prayers for one another. That is when Karen White and

Mark Williams came on board to provide their insights. Many times throughout this project, I was tested to build my own muscle of resilience and Mark Williams prayed for me. I have tears in my eyes thinking about what a gift of friendship that he has brought to me, my husband Kurt and my son Jordan.

So as I share how these incredible folks all came together, I now sit here knowing that I experienced God's grace and guidance at work. It is these people that all signed on to share their personal stories of resilience and in doing so became the wind beneath me. As you see, I thought I was a solidly rooted tree myself until the wind began to blow and shake every bit of my foundation. Even though my foundation was shaking, I am thankful to my Heavenly Father today that I was able to stand. In reflection of telling you this story I KNOW, He brought me through.

"Therefore everyone who hears these words of mine and puts them into practice is like a wise man who built his house on the rock. The rain came down, the streams rose, and the winds blew and beat against that house; yet it did not fall, because it had its foundation on the rock. But everyone who hears these words of mine and does not put them into practice is like a foolish man who built his house on sand. The rain came down, the streams rose, and the winds blew and beat against that house, and it fell with a great crash." - Matthew 7:24-27

After Christmas 2015 and the selling of my company, our family decided to move to Georgia. I personally felt I needed a fresh start. I didn't want to drive by my old office building anymore. I loved my parents and at the same time, the emotional responsibility was challenging at times. I had just gotten the first installment of payment for the sale of my company and was on schedule to receive six figures from the sale which would give me a foundation for my growing publishing and education company as well as my creative work, speaking, and media which I felt heavily called to do as a ministry. At this time our teenage son Jordan was facing his own challenges as many teenagers do and well, we all decided that moving would be a great new chapter. We had vacationed in Jekyll Island Georgia quite a bit over the last several years, and I had written down in my journal that we would have a place there someday. The first week of January we drove down to look at properties.

I was optimistic. I was holding on to the vision that 2015 was behind me. I made the decision that all of the pain, loss, and heartbreak I had experienced in that year was over. Opportunities presented themselves with me doing life, spiritual and leadership coaching and people continued to reach out to me about wanting help to become a published Author. I felt our family was on our way to leaving the past behind with a fresh start. We rented a house on five acres outside of Kingsland Georgia with a pond and an art/recording/author studio for my work. We listed our home for sale in North Carolina feeling confident. I was also scheduled to receive the next payment of my company sale which would be coming every four months. It gave the financial security that everything was coming together.

But just like weather conditions can change, the storm clouds began to thicken.

Anyone who has ever been in the beginning of a thunderstorm knows when a simple thunderstorm goes from being a sucker punch to an all-out tornadic event. I don't know how else to describe it but it was the cherry on top of what I felt was devastating to me emotionally in 2015. Mid-February rolled around, and the purchaser of our company defaulted on their schedule payment. My intuition had given me the sense they might not pay based on their previous months' actions, but I hoped that I was wrong. I wasn't.

When you are expecting six figures over a few months to hit your bank account, and you have to dip into savings, 401k and borrow money, you feel like you are holding on to the hope of it will work out. But the reality of the storm that was now brewing started to sink in. Our attorney advised that they were in default and had decided not to pay, so we needed to get our legal team together. For someone who doesn't like conflict and wants to believe the best in people it was very hard; very hard. I held on to the hope that they would honor their commitment. And yet when things didn't resolve, I had to stand strong.

Isn't that what resilience is? Standing strong even when every single thing is swirling around you in a storm that you can't control? So I stood.

During this time I was experiencing deep pain in my left shoulder (my dominant side). I had some cortisone shots a few months earlier, hoping it would improve but it got to the point I had to get an MRI. The result showed that I had a labral tear (cartilage) around the shoulder and that I needed surgery. I remember being on the phone with the insurance company getting clarity of what the bill would be because of the situation we were in. It had been years since I had struggled financially like this. I was being tested not only physically but spiritually and financially. After surgery I was told that I not only had a labral tear, I also had rotator cuff tear and bicep tear. It was a doozie. I would not even be able to start physical therapy for six weeks.

I made a decision to focus on what I could control. Some of my lifelong tools for resilience has been to write, paint, and sing. Prior to my shoulder pain, I was writing every day and doing creative art projects on the weekends. As my shoulder function diminished, my hand could no longer hold a pencil and the typing on the computer was too painful. I focused on pouring into myself in study and learning. I listened to audio books and focused on setting positive energy in motion every day in my attitude, actions and activities. Pastor Steven Furtick, ministered to me through his audio books every day and at all hours of the night. I felt I had found someone that was in alignment with my heart and mission. I watched the Elevation Church channel on You Tube that poured into my heart the teachings about how to focus your thoughts and the power of mindset. The heartbeat of my life work took stronger roots in the knowing I would deliver my experiences, the power of resilience and God's grace through my writing, speaking, singing and songwriting as well as helping other people share their encouragement through becoming published. I experienced God's provision first hand in the power of bringing people together to share their stories. They laughed and cried in conversations with me. They probably had no idea how much they were doing for my spirit. The beauty in this reflection today is God was at work during this storm.

The pain can come in such a force in the storm yet out of the pain a blessing beyond what you can imagine will be provided if you allow it. You must seek the lesson and the gift in all of it. Today I am so joyous, I am sharing this as I am literally on fire in my soul for my life.

For in August of 2014 while in Hilton Head on vacation, I had dropped to my knees and gave everything over to God to a level that I had never known so deep. I prayed out, *"God, I can't do this anymore. I give you my work. I give you my company. I give you my family. I give you my health. I give you my pain. I give you everything. I need you to handle this now."* What I know is that for him to make these changes, storms were going to be needed for the massive shift in my life. I was experiencing two parallel paths; one of amazing experiences of the spiritual gifts he was pouring into me and one of struggle and pain that I realize now was GROWTH. He was planting the seed for growth to combine with the rain of the storm so it would bring forth great things; things I just couldn't see yet.

"For I will pour water on the thirsty land, and streams on the dry ground; I will pour out my Spirit on your offspring, and my blessing on your descendants." - Isaiah 44:3

The storm changed to an "all-out" hurricane...

Two weeks after my shoulder surgery April 2016, we had a family emergency with my son resulting him going to the hospital and being there for five days. I remember that day well and every part of me shaking. Any of us that have children know that your heart can feel like it is being ripped out during moments like this. Thank God for Vickie Smith as I talked to her on the phone while standing in the parking lot of the hospital. She held me up emotionally through my tears and stood by me. Text messages from many came through with support that I needed more than ever. People joined together in prayer for my family. This is where I continued to learn the real depth of resilience and how to PRAY like never before. I can't tell you that every day I was filled with knowing that God was watching over me. Some days it was a struggle. Sometimes I wondered if He was really listening. It was in those times that unique affirmations gave encouragement to press on and I knew God was there.

Authentic friends who have real love and believe in you = resilience.

It was a couple of weeks after this experience that my husband and I talked. We were in Georgia, but we got a message indicating our house had suffered some storm damage, and it would be at least $10,000 to do the work and go through the insurance process. I remember that night thinking to myself, *"Really? How much more of this is going to continue?"* It seemed every which way we went; we hit a road block. Our son missed his hometown and wanted to be back near his friends. We couldn't continue carrying two house payments for many more months. Something had to change. We made the decision to take the home off the market and move back to North Carolina. To say it was HARD would be an understatement. I had thought we were settled. I thought this was what we were supposed to do. And now, I was questioning all my decisions that I had made over those last few months. I was asking myself questions like *"God, I understand I need to be here but why? What will my neighbors think?"* Prior to our move to Georgia, I had experienced some of the worst betrayal and friendship loss in my life as well as past memories of sexual abuse as a child (I am grateful to say that in this deep spiritual work I have been called to do that I have been freed from those chains of burden; forgiveness, understanding and empathy for those who have gone through this is now something I can bring into my coaching and teaching.) Friends that I had for over a decade, that I thought I could count on, left.

In this season of about 16 months, we had multiple scenarios of challenge. Kurt's dad went through major surgery and almost died (but they revived him) on the operating table, my father had shoulder surgery and I was faced with choosing love and forgiveness of things that happened growing up. Our camper was broken into at a storage facility for boats and recreational vehicles. Our canoe was stolen out of our waterfront marina. My sister got injured in an attack while on school property from a student (she is a teacher) and had major surgery and extensive physical and emotional therapy.

On the business side my company was thriving and my status continued to grow due to my speaking and my book gaining international attention. However, the stress of my personal hurting within my heart gave rise to physical illness and making my intuition and decision making weaker than normal. Luckily, I had my Director of Operations, Dara, who oversaw the projects and ran implementation. All ran smoothly on that end. The sales side was another story as in these moments to build revenue, I had trusted someone as a strategic partner to offer additional services to our clients. I opened my heart, my home environment, and my office to this person. During this time they wanted to buy my company of 14 years which was well established. The offer however, was they wanted to purchase the company in offering stock for their existing company. Thank goodness my husband was in those meetings and began to ask questions and research public records in regards to their company. It was uncovered that about 50% of their existing clients were one's we had helped them acquire. Their stock was worth less than a penny and after much logical thought we denied their offer to purchase us. In that decision they gained access to my company client list (database) and was prospecting our customers behind our back. It was in the middle of this that my intuition came back into focus. I am certain God placed on my heart and in my husband's mind the awareness. Both of us had been thinking (and had not shared with each other yet) that something seemed off and we should do a Google search into this person's name. Over many days of research and the hiring of a private investigator we uncovered that this person had created an alias name and had a Federal criminal record for SEC fraud; banned for life from stock trading. It was compounded even more when we tried to share this with a friend of 14 years (I thought a best friend as we talked almost every day). I had gone to her birthday events, traveled on trips with her and gave not only my heart but my business expertise to help her in all ways. It was a blow when we got a cease and desist showing her exact words that I had told her to research on her own before making any big decisions (I didn't want to disclose anything else as I was mindful of legalities). It was in that experience I couldn't even warn my clients because of the threats I was receiving. I am not exaggerating when I tell you that I feared for my safety and my families' safety after what was discovered through the investigations and court documents. That was the ultimate breaking point for me emotionally as my heart was broken so severely; into what I felt was a million little pieces. And in December of 2015 the relationship with my friend was confirmed when she said to me that our friendship had been more business than personal. I felt that I had been used all those years for my free business insight where I normally charged for it.

When we moved back into our home in North Carolina I got a knock on the door from the local sheriff. I was notified several thousand dollars' worth of jewelry was stolen by one of the movers and they had retrieved some items during another investigation in a neighboring town. The only way this was brought to my attention was my recovered high school class my full name engraved on it and the police was able to locate me easily on the search engines due to my experience in business.

During this season of storms, my resilience was strengthened. When things happened in 2015 I have to admit it, some of those days I found it difficult to even get out of bed much less talk to anyone in that season. My heart was sincerely broken and my faith had been shaken deeply. I felt alone in my faith. So, when I moved back to North Carolina where there was so much pain associated with it, this was a test of my resilience. I am so very thankful for my husband as he was and is always my strength, best friend, and provider. The gift in this storm was he began to seek God's words and prayed with me. We realized we had to go with the flow like the highs and lows of the tide. I am grateful that God was right there with me through it all. During the end of 2014 and in 2015, the friends and people that were poisonous in my life were being cleared away for me to move into God's calling on my life that I had known so many years ago. Some of these relationships were what I now recognize as co-dependent. I remember being told by my great friend Coni Meyers that our greatest strength can also be the greatest weakness. Because of my heart and having such a strong desire to be there for people (that was where I found worthiness, significance and contribution) I have been blessed to have my emails full of messages thanking me for prayers and other things to help them through.

On the flip side, it has caused great persecution in that some do not understand my heart and the calling on my life for the work God has called me to do. Even in the most recent season I was told that when I was requesting prayer on social media for a friend or raising donations for clothes for a family in need that it was to just gain attention. The hard part of these comments came from those I thought were leaders in Christ. Instead of talking on the phone with me about my "WHY" and wanting to gain understanding, they chose texting on social media to use words that were negative. The enemy tried over and over again to thwart me from standing in the gap for those in need and showing what living a Christ inspired life is all about. That is why I have a group on Facebook specifically dedicated to this as all of this has brought greater understanding to the scripture that Apostle Paul wrote in 2 Corinthians 12:10, *"That is why, for Christ's sake, I delight in weaknesses, in insults, in hardships, in persecutions, in difficulties. For when I am weak, then I am strong."*

The church I had been attending prior to Elevation Church had not felt like a fit. The day after I gave my only signed copy of *"The 21 Laws Of Leadership"* and a gift of funds to buy the pastor John Maxwell's Leadership Bible, I knew in my spirit that the

"Law of the Lid" applied in this case. My earned maturity (yes that is what resilience brings!) showed that I needed to find a church where the leader had a vision as monumental as me. As my strength in my knowing of who I was meant to be for the rest of my life my sweet friend Tracy of 15+ years invited me to Elevation Church. She had also been in a difficult season of divorce after 25 years and was working on growing her walk with God. That was another deep layer within the threads of resilient strength; strength and a mission that has grown into an unstoppable movement. Isn't it incredible that we can look back at the storm we have come from and realize what we learn from it? It is in this knowing that I am more trusting in the process because God has always carried me through. The gift in this has been the understanding of what Jesus and the disciples went through carrying the word of God throughout the land and often being criticized by those who were supposed to be of like mind and faith. It is in the knowing that others do not have your calling. They do not have your vision. They do not see what God sees in you. **They do not understand what God is doing THROUGH you!** As you see, there have been unforeseen gifts that have come to the surface in this journey. The Holy Spirit continues to strengthen my gifts that have allowed me to work intimately with those who are experiencing loss, transition, and pain in their soul; fighting to find their way back to who they were called to be.

"Very truly I tell you, whoever believes in me will do the works I have been doing, and they will do even greater things than these, because I am going to the Father. And I will do whatever you ask in my name, so that the Father may be glorified in the Son. You may ask me for anything in my name, and I will do it." - John 14:14

When the celebration and successes come, you also must know that is when the enemy will attack you. This can

make you lose momentum or just simply quit.

I remember the first few days coming back to North Carolina, after being in Georgia those short few months and questioning all of the last year. Even though I had been strong, I had a moment of inadequacy. I was wondering if I was enough; good enough; and was failing. One day while on the phone with Co-Author Mark Williams I was in the parking lot of my physical therapist after the session. I was crying. It was my first few days back to North Carolina and I felt lost. I shared with my friend what my mind was telling myself, *"Am I not moving forward now that I have moved back to North Carolina?"* All the memories of the business and personal loss were a stronger reminder here in the town where I had experienced so much. In a powerful moment he said to me something I will always remember. *"Tricia,"* he said. *"God wants you to know that you have come back as a conqueror. The reason you are back is he has more for you to do here that you don't see yet."* As I went to my church, sang, studied and worshiped I knew he was right.

With friends in my life, the resilience skills, and staying focused on God's grace of seeing me through, I often ask myself how is it that I have come through difficult chapters with such a certainty; a knowing that I will make it through? I know, and yet the word I am going to use is one that is a mystery.

It is FAITH.

Many hear the word faith and religion comes to mind. But what comes to me is having the perseverance to not give up no matter what and know that you will somehow, someway come out through the other side. Now does this mean I don't experience doubt? Of course not. Doubt is not the opposite of faith, and neither is fear.

Faith is holding on to the root and believing that even if you can't see the green above the soil that it is somehow working to create something better.

Over the years of my life, I have learned that I can't make assumptions on what should happen. Only God can direct my path. And with him, I can direct my actions, my mindset, and my attitude. Speaking of mindset however; faith is not a mindset either. We may think it is on the surface when we catch ourselves saying, *"I have faith."* What I have found that mindset does not make up the entire landscape. Without the daily action of moving forward in some way things would never have an opportunity to evolve. I think back to when I was just 19 years old. I had been working my way through college and was given the opportunity to work for a local real estate company. In that experience, I met some wonderful mentors who saw something in me and took the time to see the drive within my heart to succeed in life. I ended up buying my first investment property on my own. I was so very proud of myself to do this without even my parents knowing. I studied the classes of Dave Deldotto and Robert G. Allen. I sat at the housing office on campus at Virginia Tech and did my own interviews with potential tenants. I matched people together and filled up the rental property. I was mentored by a local real estate attorney and he had me manage his properties for him. I was so excited at the opportunity to grow in business. Being raised in a trailer most of my life except for just a couple of years, I had an intense desire to live somewhere that I could be proud of.

Then things changed. I met a young man and fell in love with him. Again, from just weeks after the start of dating, I didn't listen to the intuition that this person could be verbally abusive and have other issues. All I saw was the possibility in the future of being with someone who was getting his Engineering degree and had a strong desire for money. My craving for wanting to be loved blocked the senses of trouble that his family had experienced financial problems and possible bankruptcy. With my blinders on, I didn't think anything of it when he wanted to purchase the other rental properties with me. So, I moved forward in the process. As things in the relationship became more abusive evolving into an eating disorder and unworthiness so came the financial side of the fall as well. I won't go into the details of all of it here, but I can tell you when you walk into your home and find that everything was taken from it: the light fixtures on the walls, the washer and dryer and even the promise ring that was given (but paid for on my credit card), it can knock out almost any chance of a comeback. Thankfully, what I was able to muster in me was a faith that somehow I would find a way back to myself. If I had not had faith, I would have quit right there, but I found a way to push through the feelings of failure in my real estate ventures and get my real estate license. By the time I was 23, I was managing a real estate company office and by the time I was 27, I became the first woman National Speaker and Trainer for Realtor.com. That led to training REALTORS® on marketing and sales, being a national continuing education instructor and eventually the sales trainer for the national sales force of Realtor.com.

So as I reflect on this chapter in my life, I could not have had resilience without faith. In the book of Hebrews in the Bible it says *"Faith is the substance of all things hoped for, the evidence of things not seen."* - Hebrews 11:1 (KJV). Oh how that rang true and it is a fundamental foundation in my life. I hoped for something more. I had NO EVIDENCE of what could be at the time. My credit was ruined. I felt ugly at 5'8 and 120 pounds yet my mom was worried at my anorexia (and she had no idea of my eating disorder and the fine line of bulimia sneaking into my life). I felt like I was a failure at love. I thought I could never go into real estate since I had lost my property to foreclosure. Yet...

somehow I believed in myself; a place deep down inside me. I kept moving forward. Some days were easier than others, but I made a decision to refuse to quit but only because I held on to the provision that things would align and work out. I remember one night driving the car and thinking logically, *"If I just took my car over this mountain, all of this would go away. I would die and just not be a burden anymore and I wouldn't have to face all this pain."* Thank goodness I know God was right there with me, and he put the strength in me to persevere.

I am grateful for that as I experienced a divorce and miscarriage all within one year at the age of 26. If I had not had faith in myself, I would have not had the courage to move my life back to Virginia with little money in my pocket (and leaving my established real estate practice). I would not have seen the job posting for that National Speaker position for the internet site for the National Association of REALTORS®. I would not have had the persistence to call headquarters and ask them if they wanted to meet me in person (even though I was in VA with little resources and was offering to fly to California for the interview!). I didn't see the entire outcome of the situation at that moment. All I did was take a step of actions. After the first interview that day in California, I was offered the job. About a month later my boss and I were traveling to Palm Desert to speak to the REALTOR® Association and she said to me, *"You know why I hired you, right?"* I just looked at her not exactly knowing how to respond. *"When I was interviewing you I saw an angel standing beside you."* I thought she was crazy at that time but after my intensive angelic experience in the beginning of 2015, I know that God was revealing the higher calling, the next step of work I was to do. In writing this, I have to say THANK YOU to my Heavenly Father right now for being there for me in the darkest of storms in my life.

Faith = the cornerstone of resilience.

No wonder in the Bible there is the scripture in James 2:14, *"Faith without works is dead."* We can't sit around saying I have Faith and think it will work. We MUST to some type of work to put into action so the faith shows up. It is what I have learned to do over the trials in my life. I remember talking with a friend about the chapters in my life and she said, *"Tricia, you should write a book about how to start over because you have been so good at it with such focus and an optimistic view."*

How did I get good at it? I have put into practice ways to build my resilience in the storm. I have come to realize that without the storms there would be no rain. Without the rain, there would be no flowers. Without the flowers there would be no beautiful blooms; the blooms of opportunities; of miracles.

The gift of resilience.

The tools I had put into practice and have learned, has created the path for me to move forward more efficiently. Within days of moving back to North Carolina, doors began to open. I was now able to go back to my church with pastor, Steven Furtick, with a deeper understanding of his heart and work. I don't know the how I am to work with him in his ministry and yet I have faith because I know the WHY behind it. I feel it in every part of my being. My speaking to thousands on business, leadership, and marketing will now be on a deeper level of ministry that I was called to do when I was seven years old and again at thirteen. In the going through the storms, I am much more aware of how powerful the experience is in working with others who feel broken in their spirit. I have a deeper understanding of God's timing instead of mine. All of the combinations of experience, key relationships of other thought leaders, my speaking, writing, spiritual healing work and retreats ministry continue to present what God wants for my purpose. My publishing company and learning institute have continued to bloom out of these storms in life. I now receive the storms for I know what transformation, focus and problem solving they can bring! I get continual messages from people globally about how they have stronger faith in what they are facing. I also receive messages from CEO's that they are now sharing the vulnerability of their life journey which brings connection and authenticity to their relationships. They are building their resilience. They are inspired to keep moving forward.

If I hadn't opened the door of allowing God to work through me, these opportunities would not be here today. The vision of my life work would not be as clear as it is now.

My faith is stronger than it has ever been because I know what can be done in the midst of adversity and struggle. It is in the perseverance and the resilience in the storm that has created a blossoming of life moments for me. My family is committed to caring for one another, learning to take God's direction and truly understand what is important. Just the other day my son took my hand after church and held it. For my teenage boy to do that when most times he wants to be all grown up, my heart swelled with joy.

I find myself stronger when the storms hit, even more today than twenty years ago. You see, it grows – just like a tree in the soil. It is in those challenges that I can stand in the truth that God has me in his arms. My friends are there to pray with me and support me. My clients are there to remind me that my work is a ministry and will touch many lives for generations to come. My family is there to reaffirm what is important in this life and what needs to be most treasured. My faith and my spiritual gifts of the prophetic word give me pause to always let God lead my life instead of the other way around.

Storms always prepare us in some way for the growth that we need; even if we don't see it at the time.

Just like the tree growing in the soil, when it doesn't rain the leaves begin to wilt on the branch. When we understand that the gentle rains and the storms all contribute, it shows that it is the cycle of life and the strength of resilience.

"You heavens above, rain down my righteousness; let the clouds shower it down. Let the earth open wide, let salvation spring up, let righteousness flourish with it; I, the LORD, have created it."
- Isaiah 45:8

Strategies for Building Your Resilience

1. Practice Mindfulness - Have awareness your thoughts. Ask yourself questions that empower you.

What is the truth in front of me right now? (Ex: The truth is I have my family with me at this moment and God is here for me.)
_____
_____
_____

What can I really control? (Ex: I can control my attitude, my focus, my actions, and my mindset.)
_____
_____
_____

What do I need to release that I have no control over? (Ex: Other's perception of me, making them happy, etc.)

_____
_____
_____

What is one thing I can do to keep me moving forward; even if it just a small, baby step. (Ex: I will go for a walk and listen to a Steven Furtick message or my Audio book by Steven on Crash The Chatter Box, Elevation Worship Music, etc.)

_____
_____
_____

2. Meditate and Journal - Quiet your mind and meditate on the voice that needs to be heard. God may be trying to tell you something but you are so absorbed in the noise you can't hear it. Write your thoughts. Get them out of your head and released onto paper. It doesn't need to be perfect or seen by anyone else. Use it to work through what you need to work through in the moment.

Example writing prompts:

I am finding it hard today to feel grateful but if I had to choose just three things they would be _____, _____, and _____.

I can choose these three things because they make me realize that _____.

I feel really frustrated about _____ but I know that feeling this way will help me _____.

3. Have a creative and physical outlet - You don't have to be an artist to release creative energy. It could come in cooking a meal, or even coloring in a coloring book. Go outside to get fresh air. Take a moment to look up at the sky. This may allow you to gain a fresh perspective.

What are some hobbies where you lose yourself in time and enjoy yourself?

_____
_____
_____

When is the last time you did that?

_____
_____
_____

How could you incorporate this into your life?

_____
_____
_____

What could this do for you personally if you incorporated this more into your life?

_____
_____
_____

4. Surround yourself with an inner circle that lifts you up - People that stand by you and are there to LISTEN not necessarily give advice! Those who have faith in what can be accomplished and can lift you up when you need it most. Be careful of the relationships that drain you. You know who they are.

Who do you recognize in your inner circle that helps you through challenging times and provides you positive support?

_____
_____
_____

Who are those in your inner circle that you need to be mindful of because of the negative energy or their lack of believing in you may bring to the situation? Why?

_____
_____
_____

What could you do to improve your inner circle? (Ex: I know that going to my church Elevation, helped me along with my mentorship with John Maxwell and others that had like-minded vision.)

_____
_____
_____

How could that build your resilience when challenges come your way?

_____
_____
_____

5. Vision and/or Focus - Keep yourself on the big picture so that you hold on hope and a promise of a better tomorrow. Example: My vision of wanting to touch the hearts and lives of others has made me not give up regardless of how bleak the moment looked.

What is your big picture? What do you want to contribute to others?

_____
_____
_____

To get you through a difficult moment you can make the choice to where to focus. Just like a camera that offers different sets of lens to take that picture, you can control where your focus goes and determine if it is serving you to get you through the situation.

What are you focused on? Is this view helping you to breakthrough to the other side or is it debilitating you physically, spiritually or emotionally. What could you focus on to make things better?

_____
_____
_____

"Energy flows where attention goes."

6. Forgiveness - I had to forgive. Not just others but myself. The only way to move forward is to forgive. If you don't, it can eat you from the inside out. Ask yourself these hard questions as they will be a gateway for your breakthrough.

Who do I need to forgive in my life so that my heart and mind is free to accept new opportunities?

_____
_____
_____

What do I need to forgive myself for? Why?

_____
_____
_____

If your best friend said this to you, what would you say to them to help them release and move forward?

_____
_____
_____

7. Love - Practice self-care and surround yourself in feelings of love. One of my greatest joys has been my two dogs, Collie-mix Riley, and my Golden Retriever Gabriella. Their unconditional love always gives me comfort. My other comfort of love is in the knowing that God is there for me. All I have to do is reach out to my Bible and read those words to be reminded of his promise. Write down your insights below as this will deepen the roots of when you need to call upon resilience.

What are some situations where you felt love and connection?
_____
_____
_____

How could you bring more healthy love into your life?
_____
_____
_____

What would be some ways to love yourself more unconditionally?
_____
_____
_____

Journal this affirmation - If I put this into practice it would make me feel…
_____
_____
_____

8. Gratitude - Find something; anything in the moment to be grateful for. Seriously it could be as simple as *"I am grateful I have coffee in my pantry. I am grateful I have socks to wear."* Search for gratitude, grab it and hold on tight.

In listing my 3 things that I am grateful for I realize that…
_____
_____
_____

9. Positive words - I use positive words that I could use in the moment for moving me forward.

"God is giving me curriculum."
"The gift in this situation is…"

What could be something that you could say to yourself to reaffirm your inner strength?

_____
_____
_____

About Tricia Andreassen

Tricia Andreassen has a fire within her heart that started when she was a Youth Camp counselor at a Virginia Church of God Youth Camp; to help you grow in ways, you could never imagine. *"My mission is to bring teachings and life strategies to break-through struggles and obstacles that may arise. We all have a purpose and calling for our life and I want as many people as possible to discover what their heart calls them to do."*

Tricia's unique combination of walking this path allows her to help others fulfill their life dreams. An entrepreneur herself, Tricia bought her first real estate investment property at age 19 and has been active in the real estate industry as well as helping other industries build their brand, message and organization. Her passion for growing leaders led her to be a National Speaker and Trainer for Realtor.com®, the official internet site of the National Association of REALTORS® (NAR). After seeing a deeper need to help real estate agents and teams develop their business plan, brand, website, and marketing message, she started Pro Step Marketing from the bonus room of her house with her toddler son literally on her hip. She grew Pro Step Marketing into a leading marketing, web development coaching, and strategic planning company in the real estate niche; creating strategies and plans for over 50% of the top REALTORS® listed in production for the Wall Street Journal. After almost 15 years as CEO, she sold her company.

In 2007 another life shift happened within Tricia's soul, and she began writing songs. Her heart yearned to help others through life challenges due to her own discoveries within herself. The unlocking of this spiritual and creative heartbeat in her opened her dreams of recording her own CD, singing at a National Conference with over seven thousand in attendance, and writing her first business book which has led to writing for magazines, news organizations, personal development, and Fiction. As her journey progresses, she evangelizes the message of persistence, resilience, faith, and other life strategies with the spiritual gifts of soul healing work. Her passion is to deliver God's word and inspiration through writing books, speaking, teaching, singing, and songwriting that speak resilience and life transformation.

Over the last 25+ years she has helped thousands of people in their lives and business. One of her companies, Creative Life Publishing and Learning Institute supports this mission of helping writers become Authors as well as bringing teaching and training programs in faith, leadership, youth, parenting, business building, marketing, and spiritual growth. All the Authors published are personally interviewed and selected by her with the highest integrity. Tricia's business and marketing book hit #1 in less than 5 hours and was continually on the best-seller list for 59 weeks. She is also a Certified Speaker and Coach for the John Maxwell Organization to teach leadership, personal growth, and youth development programs as well as a Certified Executive Coach through ACTP credentials for the International Coaching Federation bringing uniquely creative strategies to work with organizations, schools, ministry groups, and leaders from all walks of life. In addition to this work she works actively through books and all communications channels to share her message.

To inquire about Tricia speaking at your next event email Tricia@TriciaAndreassen.com or visit www.TriciaAndreassen.

com. If you have a story, feel you have a message inside you, or have a desire to be an Author or Speaker please reach out to Tricia today for a confidential conversation. To book Tricia as a speaker for your next event or perhaps lead a retreat for a specific group, a call with Tricia is the first step to assure that she helps you achieve the outcome for success. Not all topics are listed on her website as some are designed custom for her clients and the specific topic of the event. Her personal passion is helping women of all ages tap into the unstoppable warrior that is within them.

Contact Tricia:
- Website: www.TriciaAndreassen.com
- LinkedIn: www.LinkedIn.com/in/triciaandreassen
- Facebook: www.Facebook.com/BeUnstoppableNow
- YouTube: www.UnstoppableWarriorWithin.net
- Twitter: www.Twitter.com/TriciaSings
- Radio Show: www.UnlockYourInnerWarrior.com

"LIFE" IN THE RING
by Chris Blackburn

LIFE" IN THE RING

"There's nothing more calming in difficult moments than knowing there's one fighting with you." - Mother Teresa

My personal definition of resilience has always been defined by taking the worst that life can throw at you, getting back on your feet, refocusing, and then to keep living the life that you are purposed to live. To be very honest, most of my adult life was without many major challenges or disappointments. I did have one brief set back in the mid-1990s when I made some poor financial choices that would ultimately lead to working two full-time jobs, a marriage in trouble, and ultimately, bankruptcy. Had it not been for the love and support of my wife, my parents, and my family, I honestly believe I would not be able to share my story.

Family has always been such a big part of my life. I have been blessed with a mother whose primary function in life was to make our house a home. I was blessed to be raised by a father who taught my brother and me what it truly means to be a man... to take care of and provide for your family at whatever cost to your own ambitions. We did not have much, but we had each other and we were happy and we knew we were loved. That was enough.

My grandparents played a huge part of my identity as well. My maternal grandmother was a Godly woman who always told me that, one day, I would become a preacher. (I spent a lot of time telling her that I was pretty sure God was calling me to be a baseball broadcaster...but she knew better). My paternal grandmother was the lady who always welcomed us with a big kiss, a big hug, and was known for making the quickest biscuits and gravy in the New River Valley of Virginia. My paternal grandfather was always a hard worker and a stickler for taking care of his vehicles. He knew a good deal when he saw one and was also a pretty shrewd salesman. I learned a lot listening to him talk and tell his stories.

Christmas was always a very special time. We would gather at my grandparent's home on Christmas Eve. Four uncles, one aunt, and a house full of cousins…all full of love, laughter, music, and of stories told over (and over…and over). To this day, I still remember the look of the old green carpet going down the stairs to the huge, refinished basement that was a concrete floor and tons of rugs to cover the floor. The walls were covered in moose and deer heads that, oddly enough, were covered in Christmas decorations. There was a tree with lights and decorations from the 1950's. The wood stove burned so hot that we would have to open the patio door to let in the chilled winter air. There was the annual gift of chocolate covered cherries and a crisp ten dollar bill. More importantly, there was always togetherness.

When we were done, we would go to my maternal grandmother's house for a more quiet time of sitting around, talking, opening a gift, and eating some small treats she made. Her Christmas tree was a small, white plastic tree that lit up and had small, ceramic bulbs inserted into open holes. She was not one for creating big get-togethers. However, she knew how to make her house a home. I still have that little Christmas tree to this day.

As I grew up, I always had my family. They were all there the night I graduated from high school in June 1988. They were there when I got married in December 1992. They were there when I was the first Blackburn to graduate from college with a four-year degree. They were there when my first son, Cole, was born and my second son, Ben. They were there when I began my career as a Sales Consultant with Premier. They were there when

Tina and I began serving in Children's Ministry at our church. They were there through success and failure. They were always there...encouraging me, teaching me, reminding me. For the first thirty-five years of my life, my identity came from my family.

Then, slowly, that began to change.

For many years, life did not throw its *"worst"* at me. Yes, there were some struggles from time to time prioritizing my wife and kids...making choices to pay bills overtaking vacations or having a bigger Christmas...not always meeting my sales goals. You know, *"Life"*. It may have seemed hard, but nothing compares to when life deals its worst hand and you are the recipient of it.

For some people, life deals its' worst in one major blow. Kind of like a Mike Tyson knockout punch you never saw coming. However, for me, it was more a fifteen round fight; a Rocky vs. Apollo Creed, type of pounding. It was an emotional and spiritual dismantling of everything I had built my life upon and surrounded myself with. Piece by piece, *"Life"* began to take my family away from me. I got my first punch in November 1999 when my uncle Cadell passed away from cancer. That was the first funeral I attended of a close family member. I vividly recall how hard we all cried as the song *"Go Rest High On That Mountain"* played. It was the first time I realized my family would never be the same. It would not be the last.

In October of 2003, my uncle Nathan died suddenly from heart failure. I was there when my dad and his other two brothers broke the news to my grandfather on the front porch of his house. My grandmother was in the early stages of Alzheimer's and he had made the decision to take care of her on his own. We were all waiting on him as he pulled into his driveway. When my uncle Anthony broke the news, my dad and my other uncle,

Gather, had to catch him as he fell. There was overwhelming emotion in me that I went to the back yard and threw up. That punch to the body was a sobering foreshadowing of the fight still yet to come.

Over the next couple of years, Tina and I began to trust God in our calling in children's ministry. I was appointed Senior Commander of our Royal Rangers ministry for boys and she was over the Missionettes ministry for girls. Our boys were involved in Royal Rangers and were playing soccer in both the fall and spring. I was traveling in three states to grow a territory that I had been assigned.

Then, *"Life"* decided to throw a solid one-two punch designed to knock me out. My grandfather's health began to fade in late 2004. A decision was made to put my grandmother in a nursing home. By this time, there were no more Christmas Eve family events at their house. I recall eating lunch after church at a local KFC on a Sunday that December with my grandfather. I was trying to encourage him about making the most of the time he had ahead. He spent his time talking about the good life he had and the life he built with my grandmother. It was his goodbye speech. In February 2005, he passed away of natural causes. My grandmother passed away 53 days later. I finished that spring with one of my worst sales performances I had in the 14 years I was with Premier. It was a very sad time, but resilience is found in taking the worst that life can throw at you, getting back on your feet, refocusing, and then keep on living the life that you are purposed to live. It was during this time that God began to deal with my heart about the spiritual fruit we are to produce when we have Christ in us.

"But the fruit of the Spirit is love, joy, peace, forbearance, kindness, goodness, faithfulness, gentleness and self-control." - Galatians 5:22-23

Regardless what *"Life"* was throwing at me, I resolved to produce these things, especially faithfulness. It would have been easy to give up ministry work and just focus on my family and my career. After all, my family was my identity. That fall, I began a new sales campaign in a newly assigned territory. It would be one of the best sales years to date. I continued in children's ministry and in serving my church where needed. However, *"Life"* found a way to throw in a great uppercut that would send me staggering, again. My mom found her mother slumped on the floor of her kitchen in mid-January 2006. For nearly ten days she was in the hospital surrounded by family and friends. My maternal grandmother passed on January 26, 2006.

I remember after her funeral talking with some of my family and friends that I no longer had any grandparents. For some strange reason, that shook me. It changed me. My identity continued to be dismantled piece by piece, round by round.

Shortly thereafter, I was offered a great opportunity to coach our local high school girls soccer team. I saw it as a great opportunity because they had not won a game in nearly ten years and I wanted to build something. I knew this would take time away from my wife and kids, but they supported my decision. I recruited girls to join the program and made promises to build a team that would compete with some of the best teams in the state…that just happened to be in our district. We created a weight-training program, a regimented practice routine, and practiced against the boys' team so that they could improve. That first season, we won two games. For most, that would have been considered failure. For me, it was a step in the right direction. That fall, we created a traveling team for the girls and then created two indoor soccer teams so that they could continue to build a more competitive team. We were becoming a family. As I write this, I see now that I was desperate to regain the identity that I had been losing.

As 2007 began, I was in the midst on my best sales year to date. I took over as the lead teacher of Life Change JV, our church's middle school aged ministry. I continued with working in children's ministry and serving in our church where needed. Our girls' soccer team had improved so much in that first year that there was actual excitement about our first game against Radford High School, a local high school from a different district. They had won the state title in the previous spring.

Our first game in 2007 was at Radford. The previous year, they had beaten us twice by scores of 9-0 and 11-0. That night, the girls played outstanding. We played some of the best-organized soccer that they had ever played. We finished regulation tied 0-0. Although the game should have ended there, we were forced to play overtime. In the second overtime period, one of the Radford players scored a goal on an amazing shot with about two minutes to play. Our girls celebrated as if we had won…and, really, we had.

I called my dad the next day to tell him about what had happened. I remember him telling me how proud that he was. Eight days later, my boys and I went to lunch with my dad and he talked to us about going on a cruise together that Christmas. He had just purchased the tickets. There was a peace about my life in that moment. After we finished, he took me to a local garage so I could pick up my car. I looked at him in the window, said I love you and told him I would call him later. It was April 10, 2007. Twelve hours later, *"Life"* threw a punch that landed on the jaw…one that was purposed to knock me out. Mom called telling me dad was in the emergency room. When I arrived, we were informed he had an aneurysm. It was massive and there would be no recovery. The next day, we had to make the decision to turn off the machines. Family and friends came to say goodbye and to offer us support. In his final minutes, my dad was surrounded by his family and our pastor. When the machines were cut off, I fell to my knees beside him, holding his hand…and I wept.

The rest of 2007 was a blur. I was numb for about six months. I was constantly worried about my mom and how she was going to hold up. Although our soccer team would win four games that year, I resigned at season's end. Simply put, I had lost my passion for coaching. I almost made my sales goal for that year, but my heart was not really in it. I continued to serve in ministry, but spent more time talking about my father and my family that I did about Jesus. You see, my identity was still found in my family.

Take the worst, get back on your feet, refocus…

My wife's mother, Cova, was now living with us. She had her leg amputated as her health deteriorated. I watched my amazing wife push through having to take care of her mother, run a day-care program, lead children's ministry, raise two boys, and deal with me and my own struggles. I could write a whole book on her. Tina is an amazing wife, mother, and daughter. I did my best to support her physically and emotionally during that time. Unlike most husbands, I loved my mother-in-law very much.

By Valentine's Day 2008, Cova's health was quickly fading and hospice was called in. I wanted to take my wife out for dinner, but that was really not an option that night. I ordered dinner from a local restaurant and brought it home for us. There was no candle-light dinner or romantic music. The next morning, I traveled for my job when my wife called to tell me that Cova had passed peacefully in our home.

There is not enough time or space to write about the mental, emotional and spiritual challenges that came after this loss. It is hard, as a man and as a husband, to not want to fix things when they are broken. I watched, helplessly at times, as my wife dealt with the loss of her mom. As a man, I felt defeated. I had no purpose and my identity was basically destroyed. *"Life"* had won…and I was ready to quit.

Take the worst, get back on your feet, and refocus...

Tina and I continued to be faithful in children's ministry and to serving our church. Our boys were about to hit the crucial high school years. All I wanted to do was duck and weave, to survive, and not take any more hits from *"Life"*. I finished the 2008 sales year just meeting my goal. I counted that as successful since other sales reps within our company were falling way short of their goal. I was being looked upon as a sales leader within our company because I was finding success in an economy that was cutting educational budgets to the core. It was something to hang my hat on. Honestly, I could have easily made a whole new identity in my career. I continued to struggle with the loss of my father…and was grieving my family. One day, while reading my Bible, I came across this scripture that really began my healing process. I found Colossians 3:1-3 and it spoke to me.

"Since, then, you have been raised with Christ, set your hearts on things above, where Christ is, seated at the right hand of God. Set your minds on things above, not on earthly things. For you died, and your life is now hidden with Christ in God."

I have always called myself a Christian. I have always tried to behave like a good Christian. However, I began to ask myself the hard questions: Do I have my identity in Chris Jesus? Are my thoughts set on those things that God has purposed for me? When I looked deep into the spiritual mirror, I answered honestly. The answer was no.

From this point, I began to focus on not just reading my Bible, but to actually study it. My prayer life began to change. My understanding of what God had planned for me as a children's pastor began to come a little clearer. My emotional wounds slowly began to heal as I began to find my identity in Christ.

I Corinthians 12:27 said, *"Now you are the body of Christ, and each one of you is a part of it."* I was a part of God's family and I had an important role to play.

"Life" was not yet done with our fight. This time, *"Life"* delivered a jab to the nose. In early September of 2008, our company sent out an unexpected e-mail stating that we would be forced to take four weeks of unpaid furlough. Basically, my family would have to survive without one month's salary. There were bills to be paid like a mortgage, two cars, utilities, and credit cards. I did what I had to do like any good father would do. I swallowed my pride and found several part-time jobs, including janitorial work. I had to make several embarrassing calls to banks to defer a car payment and house payment. Some payments were late.

I was in my office in early 2009 when it was announced that more furloughs were coming. Several of my colleagues began to talk of looking for other work. Honestly, I was scared because I loved my career, but I had to do something to provide financial stability to my family. It was then I prayed a simple prayer in my office: *"Lord, thank you for everything you have blessed me with. I thank you for my job and for helping us to get through this tough time. I got to be honest, I'm struggling right now and I'm not sure what to do. I am choosing right now to trust You. If it is my time to leave Premier, then please open the door and give me wisdom to know that it is You. If You want me to stay put, please keep the doors closed and give me wisdom to know that is You as well."*

Take the worst, get back on your feet, refocus, and keep living the life that you are purposed to live.

Nothing opened up in 2009. Furloughs came. I prayed that prayer again several months later when things got tough. In June of 2009, my oldest son nearly lost his right foot in a lawn mowing accident. *"Life"*, once again, threw a devastating punch. Our insurance covered most of the costs, but we still left with a hefty financial burden. Cole's recovery from this injury was amazing and he was not only able to walk again, but run and play basketball. God was faithful to heal.

I kept looking for other job opportunities, but nothing opened up. When I was overwhelmed with uncertainty, I prayed that same prayer and just gave it to God. In the midst of this, God was moving. I can honestly say that because of my faithfulness to everything God had called me to as a husband, father, and employee and as a servant to His ministries, God was blessing me. I was finding my identity in Christ through all of it. I was at peace.

I had great sales years in 2010, 2011, and 2012. Every year my sales went up, I gained many new clients and found myself being a leader and mentor to other sales consultants. This was accomplished despite continued furloughs and other challenges from losing my long-time sales manager and mentor, Ronnie Zindorf. Every time I saw the punches coming, my prayer remained the same. My faith was growing and I learned to just keep living the life I was purposed to live until God opened up new doors. In mid-2012, God finally opened the door.

My new sales manager and I were talking about new territory assignments in a meeting about two hours from my home. As I was driving home, I had mixed emotions about the potential to earn more money, but not really sure about the direction of my life. I prayed the same prayer again. I dropped by our church before going home and our pastor, Dr. Hal Adams, asked to speak with me privately. It was during this meeting that he told me about a potential opening for full-time employment in our before and after-school program for kids in Radford. He wanted me for that position and I felt immediate confirmation that God was opening a door...finally.

I took the worst, got back on my feet, refocused, and kept living the life that I was purposed to live . . .

It would not be until late 2013 that the position would finally open up. My final sales year was my very best. However, in December of that year, I walked through the door that God had opened and I did not look back. I was confident in my identity in Christ and knew that God had called me to minister to the children of R.O.C.K. Club and to the Radford community. Since that time, I have worked to receive my local Minister License and I believe that God has even bigger plans for me.

As I continue to study my Bible and pray consistently, I find that the Lord is faithful to reveal me those things I need to stay in the fight of ministry. Ministry offers its own life punches. God has taught me how to be resilient in a way where I know I can never really be defeated. The key is to set your thoughts on those things that God has for you, and not on the earthly things *"Life"* would have you focus on. God's ways are always better. Focus on Him and His words. When you do, you can take the worst that life can throw at you, get back on your feet, refocus, and then keep living the life you are purposed to live.

Strategies for Building Your Resilience

1. Stand tough in the midst of tough times.

When was a time in your life when you found yourself in a difficult situation?

_____
_____
_____

What mindset do you find you needed to have to get through it?

_____
_____
_____

What are some of the qualities and actions that you put into practice to stand during this situation?

_____
_____
_____

How could this understanding help you for other situations that will arise in your life? Who needs to be around you? What activities could you do to strengthen your resilience? How committed are you to this?

_____
_____
_____

2. Always…always, get back up!

When was a time in your life you were able to get back up? How did you do it?

_____
_____
_____

3. Refocus

List some ways that have helped you in the past to get refocused when needed?

_____
_____
_____

How did you gain clarity? Who did you talk to achieve that clarity?

_____
_____
_____

What is one thing you could do better to gain more focus when a difficult situation arises?

_____
_____
_____

With a heart of thankfulness, ask God to open doors for your future that He has planned for you. Ask Him to help you know when to move into the right open door.

If you did this, how could this help build your focus and your strength?

_____
_____
_____

Write what you might say to God in your conversation with him? Be open as if no one would see this but Him.

_____
_____
_____

5. Be patient! God works on His time, not ours.

What are some ways that would help you be mindful of patience and be more understanding of God's timing?

_____
_____
_____

If you find yourself getting impatient, what are some things you could do to help you through that particular moment?

_____
_____
_____

6. As you are waiting, keep living the life you were purposed to live. What does your heart call you to do when you are in a place of stillness?

When you are in the process of doing that how to do you feel? What activities could you do to help you keep moving in the direction for the life you know is what God wants for you?

About Chris Blackburn

Chris Blackburn is currently the Director of the R.O.C.K. Club children's program at the Radford Worship Center. The R.O.C.K Club provides individualized, Christ-centered care to each child who attends the program. Chris and his wife, Tina, are also the Children's Pastors at the Radford Worship Center. Chris begin serving in children's ministries in 2000 as a leader in Royal Rangers and, later, serving as Pastor over Life Change JV, a pre-teen youth ministry.

Chris has a passion for young people that took flight in 2001 when he was hired by Premier, A School Specialty Company's Planning and Student Development division as a Sales Consultant to schools in Virginia, West Virginia, Kentucky and Tennessee. His consulting work helped implement programs into many schools that included *"The 7 Habits of Highly Effective Teens"*, *"The Leader In Me"*, and *"The Go Program"* among others. Chris specialized inteacher-focused in-services and staff development. Twice, Chris was named to the President's Club by Premier for achieving higher than projected sales goals.

Chris has been invited on an annual basis since 2010 to be a key speaker at the Virginia Future Business Leaders of America summer conference.

Chris's earlier business experience came as a contract supervisor for Defender Services, Inc. on the campus at Virginia Tech to provide custodial and maintenance for rental properties. There, Chris hired and trained employees from various employment agencies. During his tenure of six years, he had the lowest employee turnover rate. This was an amazing accomplishment considering these employees received minimal wages and no state benefits.

Chris's passion is to help people achieve their potential through encouragement, vision and through their faith in God. He believes that the best way to achieve this is to be honest, but in a loving way.

Contact Chris:
- Website: www.RockClubVA.com
- Email: 19ChristopherBlackburn@gmail.com

LOOKING IN THE MIRROR
by Janet DiTroia

LOOKING IN THE MIRROR

"I'm starting with the man in the mirror. I'm asking him to change his ways. And no message could have been any clearer. If you wanna' make the world a better place, take a look at yourself, and then make a change." - Michael Jackson

Have you looked in the mirror lately? Now I don't mean during the simple daily routines such as combing your hair, applying your makeup or brushing your teeth. For these are the typical tasks that we unconsciously do every day. What I am referring to is the deep introspection into those beautiful eyes. It's that window to your gentle soul. It's the all-knowing, delicate, powerful, graceful child that lies within you. Now for the burning question, do you see an image you love? Do you feel love radiate through your very being when you gaze closer into that mirror? And, most importantly does it say back "I love you?"

It can be so difficult at times, especially when you don't seem to like, let alone love, what you see in the mirror. We all have beliefs and behaviors which have led us to act in certain ways or to believe things about ourselves. Perspectives and perceptions are the driving force for our every breath. This is the very fabric of why so many people find it hard to love themselves. We have misunderstood our true divine nature.

We have forgotten the very essence of who we are.

For over 40+ years I can remember not even wanting to look in my eyes. It was just too painful. I could hear a voice say, *"What an ugly nose. Your eyebrows are too light. You have to squint to see - go put on your glasses on."* Or *"You look to fat in those clothes."* Does anything like this sound hauntingly familiar to you? Unfortunately, it is something we all can relate to. We misunderstand our intrinsic beauty and our powerful presence. We unconsciously say things to ourselves that we would never say to someone else. We can be so cruel and downright disrespectful towards the innocent fragile child that lies underneath all of our pain from the past. Not realizing this, over time we siphon off the good things coming to us because we do not feel deserving, worthy, valued, and most of all loved.

Many of our beliefs come from our childhood…

I can only speak for myself here, but I spent many years being bullied by people who I thought were my friends. I dreaded going to school and cried all the time. I wondered, *"What was wrong with me?"* This continual cruelty went on throughout my high school years. In fact, my whole family was treated disrespectfully by some families and kids in the neighborhood. Everywhere I seemed to go I was consistently reminded of how I smelled, couldn't see and looked like *"a dog."* In my sadness, I unknowingly gave away my power which led to very low self-esteem. I didn't know how to handle my *"Overly Sensitive Emotions"* (as a Psychic I had not realized my true innate powers) so I sank deeply into helplessness, hopelessness, and heartache. My family was frustrated and did not know how to deal with all of the ongoing aggravation throughout the years. Since we all suffered together it was really hard to see outside of the box of misery for myself and for my family.

I carried this emotional pain well into my forties.

Within my marriage of twenty-nine years and three beautiful children, I wanted to just give up, more times than I can count. I didn't love myself. I didn't know what loving yourself meant. I truly know my parents did the best they could in helping me to manage in my teenage years as they were also sad and hurting.

It is no wonder why I had reoccurring dreams about drowning. I guess I felt as if I was drowning in my life, I felt defeated.

Where was inner strength, my resiliency? Had I lost it all? Or better yet, did I even have it to begin with? I kept asking myself *"Is this what my life is supposed to be about?"* I questioned everything. On one of my darkest days, I heard a voice telling me, to peel the layers of misery apart, *"It's time Janet. My dear sweet child, your life is not meant to be like this."*

So who was this talking to me?

I heard it on the inside and this was weird to me at the time. I have now come to realize it was God (you may call it intuition, source, creator, my higher self, etc.). Somehow…someway…I finally I listened…I now call this moment of realization my *"Resiliency of Spirit."* Unwavering in LOVE, I believe my spirit was telling me to never give up on me. It was in that very moment of revelation my inner world literally exploded into pieces.

I started to pick up each piece of me. I had to figure out why I felt the way I did. I had to sit quietly and reflect on ways of to how to deal with the pain that had been layered on for many years. It took me quite some time to sift through the experiences so I could process, gain understanding and integrate why it all happened. I realized that there was to be no more holding of all this stuff in my head. The fear, doubt, hurt, disrespect, frustration, and unworthiness were emotionally exhausting and it was not helping me to move forward. Over this time, I evolved; never to be the same.

In the process, I did find one consistent truth in everything I read. It said that:

We are beings of love and light here to remember, reveal, express, demonstrate, and be the best that we are meant to be with every single breath we take...

The flame deep within me began to brightly shine. What had been within was not anymore. So much so that at age 47 I decided to write a book about it, called *"My Eyes are Open."* It was in that realization that I finally came out of hiding to remember who I really am. I now choose to celebrate, honor, and welcome all of my past painful experiences as they are the true foundation of my gifts. They have brought me right here to you-all graciously and lovingly realized. Thank you for allowing me to share them with you.

In this moment...

It is important to understand that everyone has their own sense of how they see themselves. It is based on many years of experiences all of which penetrate deeply within everyone's mind of subconscious programming. Yes, life happens, but, when you realize it's how we react to our life experiences that determine our happiness and well-being, your take on life is much different. I didn't realize these golden nuggets of wisdom till later on in life. These pearls of love are here for all of us. They come forth through our intuition, our dreams, a gentle voice in mediation, prayer, or those quiet moments of stillness. These words are here to provide graceful guidance for helping us to remember who we really are. It is through learning, expanding, and growing in our mind, body, and spirit.

I have been reading, writing, teaching, and attending seminars. Many times I speak on the topic of *"love"* as I am committed to helping others unravel their own truth. When we love, accept, approve, validate, honor, and respect ourselves we do not fall prey to the unconscious illusions we may have once believed to be true. You know the ones. It is those that don't make us feel empowered or uplifted. Essentially, it is the stuff that doesn't make you feel happy.

When we do not fully realize our greatness, we rob ourselves of our good. We unconsciously live in that reality created through our experiences each and every moment. When we unfold the real truth, however, our perspectives and perceptions are greatly affected in beautiful ways. I feel very confident in saying there is not one specific reason why many of us do not know how to love ourselves as it is a culmination of things. But one underlying common thread remains to be seen and that is, *"We haven't truly embraced who we really are."* We may think we know ourselves, as I thought I did, but it was a false façade of my outer experiences reflecting back at me and not what was truly in my heart.

In essence, I had it backwards like many of us. Our inner essence (our intuition) will always have our best interest at heart no matter what. If we make our decisions in life from looking on the outside for our answers, we will never come to peace with loving ourselves fully. I traveled that road a long time and it became tiring and unfulfilling, to say the least. We all deserve better, much better.

Learn to listen to your best friend, you, for no one except God can love you more than you. Embodying these words will provide to the best foundation for any resiliency in life!

For so long the image that I looked at in the mirror was misunderstood and misguided by my own beliefs, the negative thoughts and the patterns that were developed over time. My understanding was clearly the culmination of everybody else's thoughts, actions, and words. There is no blame. It is the awareness of the truth for me. I believe we are all children of this *"Grand Universe"* given no rule books, and little directions about unconditionally loving ourselves. Here on this earthly plain, our experiences are guided to give us many varied opportunities to grow, learn from, and expand to our highest potential. Some experiences are more painful than others. I can only relate to my pain and how it impacted me for a long time. Now I see these as blessings! Yes! They are all opportunities. It allows for evaluation and the unfolding of the situation. It provides insight into what you can take away from each and every circumstance.

With each breath I take and no matter what has happened along the way, I have come to realize that it has been guided into a delicately woven fabric of life. Think about it. This it is YOUR time to uncover *"the real deal, the crème da la crème."* It's time to discover the complete picture of your existence.

Love is and, always will be the answer to everything.

Do you have a story about your experiences that have led you to feel the way you do about yourself? We all do. Just know the past can't change *BUT* your reaction to it *CAN*. Use these blessings as a way to guide you, and uncover your divine nature with grace to gently move you forward with strength, resilience, and an inner confidence that you are deserving of the best life has to offer. What can you do to help yourself crack open your layers in life so you can better embrace and love yourself more fully and completely?

I went on a journey to find out, and that was a big part of my inner healing. It didn't happen overnight. However, with patience, and an unwavering commitment to myself as well as a willingness to want something much better I stepped out. I took each day with a day-to-day mentality to now living passionately moment to moment.

So what did I do to shift myself?

I embraced the true me through writing books, speaking, and working with charitable organizations. I also took walks in the park, connected with nature, and learned to cultivate meditation. I read books about beauty in and around the world. I visited sacred places in my imagination and in person to expand my vision and understanding of life.

Probably the most difficult part came next. I spent time looking at pictures of myself as a young child and telling my inner child everything she needed to hear in order for *"her"* to feel complete and loved, (you may want to have a tissue box close by for this) it was one of the most difficult things I had to do. This whole process was completely liberating. I also now make it a common sincere practice of telling others I love them just because. . .it makes them feel special and I get to give a gift of love that is so powerful.

In the past, I looked at the image in the mirror because I had to. Today I look at the image in the mirror because *I WANT TO*. I am strong and resilient. I am fearless to speak my mind with compassion and love. I enjoy being with myself and I honor how I feel on a moment to moment basis. I respect, love, approve, validate, and accept myself unconditionally, and that is a breath of fresh air for this girl. I am consciously living my life from this point forward from a heart-centered consciousness.

Would you consider looking in the mirror and seeing the beautiful child within?

What would you have to lose by beginning and ending each day with "I love you"? Not only would you feel good, you will begin to open the door of self-love, and that is powerful!

Over time you will gently shift and allow yourself to step into the magnificence of who you truly are. Just as a pebble dropped in a lake can affect all of the surrounding water, you can help the world change in wonderful ways with one *"I love you"* at a time…and it all starts with each of us. Are we willing to unveil the real truth about who we really are? I surely hope so. I love you and I honor you for taking the first step.

Strategies for Building Your Resilience

1. Do you have a story about your experiences that have led you to feel the way you do about yourself?

_____
_____
_____

2. Gather pictures of yourself from your childhood. What would you say to that child today? What would you want them to know that they may not understand yet? (You may need a box of tissues for this. I did!)

_____
_____
_____

3. Take some time and look in the mirror. What could you say to yourself that would help you uncover and remind the beautiful things about yourself?

_____
_____
_____

4. If you began talking to yourself like you do with your very best friend or your own child who you adore, how would that change your life?

_____
_____
_____

About Janet DiTroia

My mission is to embrace, love, acknowledge and empower every child as a unique expression of love, knowing that everyone of us has exquisite gifts to be brought forth in miraculous ways. As a conduit of God's loving light may I guide our own inner child and the children who grace our presence to embody the truth: that we all matter, and are magnificent beings here with passion and purpose to shine brightly with all our dreams to become true leaders in a world created through the grace of love, peace and joy honoring our hearts completely with a genuine respect for all living things.

May we all walk together as one...

Contact Janet:
- Website: www.JanetDitroia.com

SUICIDE IS NEVER THE ANSWER
by Jordan Andreassen

SUICIDE IS NEVER THE ANSWER

My mom asked me to be in this book, but I am not a writer. I am a gamer (My dad says I'm addicted), a debater (yes, I like to argue or get out of chores – what teenager doesn't!), and a pretty quiet guy to most people. But when my mom and I talked more about it, I figured that if I didn't share my story that there might be some kid out there having a day like I had. If I can save just one life by sharing this painful story with you then I will, even if it is a bit uncomfortable. I want to acknowledge my mom for helping me get this written down as she is more of the writer in the family.

This message is for kids and for the parents of those kids.

It was my 6th grade school year; a tough year going to a new school much bigger than my elementary school and trying to fit in. And on most of those days, I definitely didn't feel like I fit in but I didn't tell my mom and dad about the days that were tough. I was trying to forget about some of the days by ignoring my feelings and focusing on video games and watching YouTube channels. I even went to sites that I shouldn't have based off trying to fit in more with my peers. It was my escape from my feelings.

But, some days even that didn't work. Some days were just down right terrible. I rode the bus in my neighborhood and I had faced a problem every day getting on that bus. There was another kid in my neighborhood that was in the only group of friends that I actually felt like I could sit with. We had started out as best friends and I trusted him because of that and then things changed where he didn't like me. I think back to it and it might have been over liking the same girl or something. It was something so trivial honestly. But what wasn't trivial was what I experienced. You see, that experience shaped a lot of my actions and thoughts which will go into my adulthood.

When I was at school one day, this boy started saying things to me. I tried to hold my own and act strong in front of those who were listening. Most times I could push off things but then he said something I won't forget. *"Why don't you just go home and kill yourself."* It was awful. As I was on the bus, the thoughts ran through my mind and I actually started to believe what he told me. It brought so much pain to me that I came in the door and went up to my room. I didn't tell my mom when I came in the door. I just didn't talk at all and went up to my room. While there on my bed, I made a decision that I was going to take my life. I gave in to the thoughts of *"I am a loser. I have no friends. No one likes me…"* So, I began to think about how I was going to do it. Thank God, I know that he was watching over me because it was during those moments my friend Brooks reached out to me and said, *"Hey, you want to hang out?"*

If it wasn't for that text from Brooks in those moments I would have lost all hope and done something that I couldn't take back. Because of the pain inside, I wasn't thinking rationally at all. And, what I now realize is there are many kids and even young adults that contemplate taking their life. According to www.BullyingStatistics.com there is a link between bullying and suicide and I can relate to that. When we are growing up, our identity often relates to what others perceive of us instead of how we see ourselves. I think that is natural because we are probably still coming into our own, and finding who we are as a person. We look to those around us to give us solidification of that. According to statistics reported by ABC News, nearly 30 percent of students are either bullies or victims of bullying, and 160,000 kids stay home from school every day because of fear of bullying.[1] It also says that over 14% of high school students contemplate suicide at some point.

It makes me wonder what the percentage is for those in middle school. I only say that because from my experience Middle school was a difficult time for me. I went from pretty much straight A's to B's and C's. My mom talked to my teacher and she told my mom how reserved I was in class and didn't talk much. Up until a year or two ago that was more the case but as I have matured and improved my communication skills that has changed. In writing this I discovered that girls between the ages of 10-14 have even a higher risk of suicide. Statistics show that suicide results in 4,400 deaths per year.

I think that is why I decided to share this. My mom had no idea until a couple of summers later when we went camping in Cherokee North Carolina. I ask my friend Brooks if he wanted to come along for the trip. We were sightseeing one day. While I was in the back seat I happen to tell Brooks about it and said to him, *"You know you saved my life that day didn't you?"* My mom and dad were in the front seat and overheard. We talked a little bit about it but not much as I didn't want to talk about it too much. It was only until I became a John Maxwell Certified Leadership Speaker that I shared my story more openly. We had an exercise where we had 5 minutes to share our personal story and I opened up and started to share with the people around me. Everyone at the table was all adults. In fact, out of over 3 thousand people in the room, I was the youngest person there. I have been told I'm either the youngest (or 2nd youngest) certified coach and trainer in the world. I met an incredible mentor Mark Williams who has had several calls with me to talk to me about life and I also met a friend Pat Gano who inspired me because in her 80's she is still going strong in going to classes and learning. During this conference I heard Nick Vujicic share his message of his disability of having no arms and legs. He shared about the day he also thought of attempting to take his life in the bathtub and also making a decision to make his life mean something despite his challenges. At the conference I had the ability to meet him backstage for a few minutes before speaking in another session. It was inspiring and transformational to see what a person can accomplish at any age in their life. My hope is to work with Nick some day and have him as my personal mentor. So Nick if you read this, I am ready!

This is why I share in this book about resilience.

If I had not made it through that dark moment I would not have the awesome experiences I have experienced. I am grateful that it came up, in the truck that day, with Brooks and my parents overhearing. My mom knew intuitively something was off but because I didn't discuss things she couldn't figure it out. Luckily she read into me and got me enrolled in a private Christian school about 30 minutes from our house. I have to tell you that it was a catalyst to changing my life. I remember the day she took me there before the start of the school year and saying to her, *"Mom I am so happy I could cry right now."* I know, I know, that might not be a guy thing to say but it is how I felt. I was so happy I could put that behind me and have a fresh start.

And I did. I had an incredible Principle Ms. Kathy Keane and some incredible teachers that encouraged me and saw the good inside me that I never believed in before. That was a turning point and my grades bounced back up honor roll level. At the end of 7th grade I took some testing and I scored really high on those tests in all categories over 95%-99% of top statistics. I went to a summer camp and over that time matured a lot. When I returned from school I talked to my principal about skipping a grade as my studies came so easily to me. She agreed reluctantly telling me, *"Jordan, I have only approved this once in 22 years of being an educator."* I started believing in myself instead of looking to kids for approval. I started realizing that to fit in I would have to act like everyone else and not stand out. It was in the combination of my school leaders and the John Maxwell organization that showed me that I was meant to be unique. It was okay not to fit in to the masses. It made me feel a lot better. My whole life (yes, I know I am just 15 right now), I have actually had a better connection with people older than me. Maybe it's because I am an only child. My aunt Karen (Gigi, my mom's sister) says that mom was like that too. Some of my favorite days are when I can hang out with my '3rd set, adopted grandparents, Grammy and Mr. Rick. Those days talking and visiting together are some of the most incredible days of my life.

I say this because when I came home from school that day I didn't really think through all the incredible people in my life that loved me so much: MorMor (Danish for grandma), Poppy (who thankfully I was by his side at his recent passing), Grandma, Grandpa, Grammy, Mr. Rick, Gigi, Uncle Jimmy, my friends like Brooks, and my parents. I had been so clouded in the moment I couldn't see anything put pain and hopelessness. I couldn't imagine things getting better. But I am here putting this down in a book where everyone can read telling you this:

Things will get better if you allow it.

You have to reach out to someone you trust. Shoot, if you don't think there is anyone right now message me on Instagram (@JordanAndreassen) or email me on my page at www.JordanAndreassen.com. I never want you to feel like you don't have someone out there that doesn't understand you. Trust me I do. I think about 6th grade and remembering another experience. One of the other students in my neighborhood was having a going away party as they were moving. My friend Brooks was invited but I wasn't. When I reached out to the kid, he said he didn't invite me because he didn't want me to get bullied there. That was a huge punch in the gut.

But you know what? I saw something that changed me for the better.

My friend Brooks stood by me in friendship. He said, "*If you can't go to the party, I'm not going to go ether.*" Brooks probably wouldn't call himself a leader but he was just by doing that. He led with his actions and was intentional in helping me feel better.

Now, here I am sharing this message and I want to be clear my moments are not perfect. I still have issues on things. I argue with my Dad often because I feel like he doesn't understand me. I am not the best on doing chores in the time they are supposed to be done. I procrastinate at times. But, one thing I know; there is a God and he cares about me. Regardless if you believe in God or not, there is always someone who cares about you. I used to be an atheist when I was in 6th grade. I seriously didn't believe that there was a God even though my mom was a believer. However, an experience with my Grandma changed that. (That could be a whole other story for another time). I started to see so much easier than before. My conversations with my mom developed deeper and she helped me learn how to pray or talk things out at times when they were tough; even when I didn't believe in prayer. It is what has been a help to me even though I wonder at times if prayer works and I question things. I am still growing and learning but now I have mentors that I can look up to and help me realize the possibility in my life; my present; my future.

Strategies for Building Your Resilience

1. Have a list or even if it is just one or two people that you trust that you can confide in. If you are in a moment where you don't feel like you have anyone, reach out to a school counselor or a church pastor; even me. I promise even when it seems dark there is someone out there who cares about you.

Who comes to your mind that you could reach out to in times that are overwhelming?

_____

_____

_____

2. Talk to your parents. I know there may be an exception for some of you where you have a parent who is in addiction, abuse or perhaps you have no parent. You may feel angry or misunderstood but if you have a parent know that they love you. It starts with talking and building trust between the two of you.

When is the last time you had a one-on-one conversation with your mom or dad? How did it go? What could you do different to make the experience even better (maybe going out for a walk, making a dinner together, doing a sport together, etc.)

_____

_____

_____

3. Have you ever had a day when it is seemed hopeless and in the following days things seemed to get better? What got you through those days? How could you take these tools to make your life better?

_____
_____
_____

FOR PARENTS:

1. When is the last time you scheduled out a specific time to do something special in a one-on-one environment with your child? I say this because I can connect deeper when I have alone time with my mom or my dad. Recognize we need this bonding time.

_____
_____
_____

2. What are 3 things that your child is passionate about? What have you learned about their personality based on these interests?

_____
_____
_____

3. After hearing my story, what comes to your mind about your child? What could you do to be more aware in their day-to-day life?

_____
_____
_____

[1] Source statistics from BullyingStatistics.com

About Jordan Andreassen

Jordan Andreassen is a high school student in the Charlotte NC area. His hobbies include video gaming, marketing, making videos, politics, and history.

In 2016 at the age of 14 Jordan became a Certified John Maxwell Speaker and Trainer that allows him to teach and conduct training sessions on life and leadership. He is the #1 or #2 youngest certified trainer for John Maxwell worldwide. His focus is on giving encouragement and bringing awareness to youth issues such as bullying, self-esteem issues, peer pressure, and depression. He also believes that being a leader can start at any age and enjoys bringing leadership strategies to youth.

Inquire about having Jordan conduct a special session at your school, youth camp, church youth group, summer camp, YMCA or other youth related conferences please visit www.JordanAndreassen.com and fill out the contact form.

Contact Jordan
- Website: www.JordanAndreassen.com
- Instagram: www.Instagram.com/JordanAndreassen

GIVING IT TO GOD
by Cindy Lea

GIVING IT TO GOD

"The Lord is my strength and my defense; he has become my salvation."
– Psalm 118:14

My story of resilience starts as a far back as when I was a child in my mother's womb. My mother was in an abusive relationship with one child in hand, and another one on the way. She never knew what would set my dad off. It was often something as little as not having ketchup in the cabinet. He was a very angry person and would take that out on my mother. I don't remember him ever taking things out on me except for one time. It was the night my mom left my dad for good when I was around 3 years old.

As I was growing up, my mom did not tell me about any of the bad times. She would never speak badly of my dad, even when when he did not stop by on our birthdays or come to school or church functions. She always made up excuses for him. So that led me to believe that he was needed somewhere else and it was ok, because he was saving lives or finding criminals. It was normal to us for him to not be around but we made do. I always knew that I was a fighter. I didn't know why until my mom told me that when she was pregnant with me, my dad abused her and would hit her while I was in her stomach. So that's when my fighting and being resilient started; right in the womb and it has never stopped.

Even on the days I feel like lying down and just giving up, the voice in my head says, "Get up and move on; you've got this."

My mom is the greatest. She sacrificed so much for her two kids. We are who we are today because of her. She never let anything get her down, or if she did we never saw it. It seemed like she could turn a penny into a dollar and always give us what we needed. I never remember feeling bad about not having what others had. We got what we needed and it was enough. I loved our once a month walk to get pizza. It was such a treat for us: me, my brother, and mom, walked from our apartment to eat pizza at a buffet place. It was the greatest adventure ever to us at the time.

I never remember being hungry. I just remember looking in the cabinets and not seeing a lot to eat. I do remember asking my mom why she wasn't eating. She told me she wasn't hungry. Now that I am older, I know she was hungry but she just wanted to make sure the two of us had enough to eat. She always made the ultimate sacrifice for us kids and I never will forget it. She is the strongest person I know, and I am glad that I am a chip off the ole' block so to speak, if I am half as strong as her! And yet, that is the reason I have been through so much and have bounced back from everything.

All my life I have seemed to have bad things happen to me. I don't dwell on them. I just deal with them and go on. I've learned that if you get knocked down, get back up. It doesn't matter how many times; you just do it. Some people might say I'm stubborn, but that's ok, because I'm strong. I get stronger after overcoming each obstacle. We are designed by God to learn from our struggles. He puts things in our path for a reason. He wants us to see what will happen when we do not let the enemy get to us. This is easier said than done sometimes. Often throwing in the towel would be so much easier, but what would you learn? Nothing is easier than giving up than to give it to God and let him handle the situation.

You must not give up because greatness for you is just around the bend.

One of the most comforting things I have ever learned is to give it up in prayer. Then, just let it work out the way God intends it to happen. This can work for many situations: family, relationships, illnesses, anything. I have some examples of my faith in the midst of illness. As a child, I was sick with kidney issues. It is not something now that I even remember clearly. The only thing I remember is my mom, grandparents, brother, and uncle being there. I remember one painful shot and how horrible the food was while I was in the hospital after a surgery. I don't have to remember how painful anything was because the pain was only there for a little while. Surgery repaired the problem and I went on my way. At that age did I know that God would have the doctors do the right procedure to heal me? Not really, but I do know my grandparents were praying and believing so I didn't worry about anything.

As an adult, I became very sick at the end of my 20's. I had lost 40 pounds in just a couple of months. I knew something was wrong. I went to doctor after doctor not getting answers but getting sicker. Finally, one day I asked God, *"Please send me where I need to go and see what is wrong with me."* A person at work had a glucose meter, and I asked him to check my blood sugar. He did, and my blood sugar was over 300, so I knew to call the doctor and to be checked specifically for that. God put that person in my mind to ask and pointed me in the right direction.

It's amazing when we become quiet with God and just listen.

Within a day I had an appointment at my doctor's office again. This time it was with a person who specialized in diabetes. Again

I was poked for blood. When the nurse practitioner came back in the room, she had some nurses with her and said to me, *"Tell us how you are feeling."* I remember the conversation even to this day some 16 years later. I told her, *"Well my stomach hurts, that's about it."* She looked at me and told me and the other nurses that my blood sugar was well over 600 and that I was a walking miracle. When she gave me a shot of insulin to make my sugar come down, I felt amazing and like I hadn't been sick at all. God put one person in my path to make it to the path I needed to be on. I was treated with no complications. I had been diabetic with very high blood sugars for over four months. I had no complications from the sugars, which is a miracle in itself.

Sadly, it didn't last long. One day I was home very sick. I had never been that sick in my life. I called the Doctor on call and got some tips, and ended up having to call him back. He said, *"Come on to the hospital."* I called my then husband to take me to the hospital. It wasn't a good ride to the hospital, but I needed to go. My first husband and I didn't have a good relationship at that point. It seemed like he didn't care at all if I was sick, dying, or alive. He proved that later on at the hospital. I got to the hospital where my mom and brother were waiting for me. I was so glad to see them. My mom went back with me and the doctors told me that I was in Diabetic Ketoacidosis. I had no idea what they were talking about. They kept saying I was a type 1 Diabetic, when I told them I was a type 2. I was so sick; I had to be put in ICU. I didn't even realize I was that sick. My body was trying to turn on itself. They put me on an IV drip of insulin, and all kinds of medications.

I remember feeling so much better when they got the pain in my stomach to stop. Everyone left me for the night. I didn't expect my husband to stay anyway, because of the way he was acting. I was really too sick to care. I knew my mom would take care of me and I didn't worry. I didn't have any type of feeling that I was going to die. I just felt that I was sick and they were going to make me better. Later that night, I heard a bunch of alarms going off. It was very hard to sleep with all the buzzing away. But when the nurses started running around getting a cart, my first thought was *"Oh, my! Someone is in here dying tonight. This is such a shame."* In that moment I said a prayer.

They were coming into my room. I looked at them, very puzzled. They said, *"Your blood pressure dropped and we got alarmed. We need to check the equipment."* Sure enough there wasn't anything wrong with the equipment. My blood pressure had dropped to 50 over 30. They kept me on watch all night long. I had to stay there a couple of days and finally was released. I was so tired and drained.

I knew I had some things in my life that needed to change.

I realized that I could have died and I was not happy with what was going on in my life right then. I would have been so sad if that is how my life would have ended. It brought awareness that there were some very harsh people in my life. At checkout, my husband picked me up and took me home. On the ride home, he told me his family was coming over and he had left the house just like it was when I went to the hospital. He went on to say that if I didn't want to get embarrassed by the house, I had better clean it up before they got there. I was shocked and stunned; I didn't even remember anything he was talking about. What mess? When I got home, the breakfast that I had made three days earlier was still there. He left all the pans on the stove, and everything was just like I left it. I was so sick and now depressed. I had gotten up that morning while sick to make his breakfast to take to work. My thoughts began to swell. Here I had been sick and in the hospital and he couldn't even clean up the stove. I was so mad, tired and frustrated. I was feeling every bad emotion possible. I couldn't believe it. I knew I had married someone who was cruel and unloving for sure. Our marriage ended a little after that. We were going to try to have a child, but we were unable to. A child would have made me extremely happy to have him or her, but I'm so glad that I didn't have that to deal with in addition to dealing with him.

I had to start over...fast.

The night I left, he raised a hand to me and that was something that was never going to happen to me. Unfortunately, I had let him belittle me but hitting me was one thing I would never let happen. I guess that brought back painful childhood memories. I left that night in the wee hours of the morning with snow pouring down. I still to this day do not remember getting out of one of our back bedrooms and down the steps. I was on a downward spiral with relationships where I let people belittle me, tell me what I could wear, follow, and watch me to make sure I was working, but would lie and cheat themselves. Finally, I had to do something for me; for the little that was left of me. After years and years of relationships with the wrong kind of person, I finally took control of my life.

One of my good friends had joined a dating site. She told me to go on this particular site and see if I would look into it. I remember her telling me, *"You don't have to do anything. Just get out and meet people; go out to eat."* Well I did for a little bit, but I didn't like it at all. I thought to myself *"Here I am, I'm going to end up on the news, local woman meets man from the internet and is missing."*

Finally, I said a prayer.

I remember it word for word. *"God, I said, "I'm giving this to you. I am obviously not doing a good job at finding the right person. So from now on I'm giving it to you and your timing."*

Well, I didn't have to wait long. That night when I got home, I logged on to the dating site to remove my profile. At that time a message showed from guy I didn't know. I thought, *"Oh my goodness, I can't seem to get off this website."* But something told me to answer him. We talked and exchanged texts. I never got on the site again after that connection. He was logging on for the first time to this site, and I was logging on for the last time. God didn't make me wait long, but it wasn't until I gave it to him that it happened. I know that it wasn't just God that had a hand it in. I know that my Grandpa was standing there saying, *"Okay, it's time. Go ahead and let them meet."* My grandfather had died on a Valentine's Day right after he had made my grandmother a handmade heart. From then on I hated Valentine's Day. It always made me think of his death. I know that my grandfather didn't want me to think like that anymore. My first date with my now husband was on Valentine's Day.

Four and a half months later, we got married. Some people say that was too fast. But through a lot of trials and things that have happened in our lives we are still standing tall. We have our family going to church and have become a more faithful family, when trials come our way. I just stand back and go to a quiet place and put the word up. *"Dear Lord, I am giving this issue to you, I do not want to worry about things that I cannot control, only you can control this situation."* I give it to God.

No matter all the health issues or risks I have faced, some of them even before birth, I'm still standing. I'm still able to receive blessings, many times through the hardships. The blessings still come even through tears. I will never give up. I'm here for a purpose. Sometimes God clearly shows me my purpose and sometimes I have to wait to hear what I am supposed to do.

No matter how you are feeling at this moment, no matter what is going on bad or good, God is there in the background working and moving on the situation. Don't try to counteract what he is working out for you.

In one of my recent family situations, one of my friends prayed for our situation and prayed for things to be revealed so that things would be clearly seen. Within one day of an approaching court situation for custody, things came out that made everything so clear. It was God and the prayers of others that helped make the situation clearer for the people who had to make decisions, because of this simple prayer. We trust in God, and we go on day to day. We trust in God for our situations we face and know that he is always with us working on his plans.

Strategies for Building Your Resilience

1. Trust in God's timing. What could you do to turn it over to Him and learn to trust him?

_____
_____
_____

2. Give your troubles and concerns to God and then let go of them. He has it under control. What are some of these issues that you need to release to Him?

_____
_____
_____

3. You will find peace if you do not worry about something you cannot control. How would your day change if you no longer had to worry about these things? How would that change your relationships? Work? Life?

_____
_____
_____

4. When things happen in your life, sit back and reflect. What am I to learn from this experience, how am I supposed to grow? Ask God to show you what you are supposed to do with this situation.

_____
_____
_____

Are you going through a situation right now? How could you put these above mentions into practice?

_____
_____
_____

5. When God puts you in a situation, it is for you to learn something, either about yourself or someone close to you, or he is going to give you the tools to help someone else?

_____
_____
_____

6. Think about a time when you dealt with a challenge and you ended up learning something that helped you long term. What was the situation and what did you take away from the experience?

_____
_____
_____

About Cindy Lea

Cindy was born in southwest Virginia, where she has made her home with her husband and step-daughters. They live in a small community that is very peaceful; near a lake and the New River. "The drive to work and home is very peaceful, as I cross the lake and revel in the wonder of Gods beauty."

Cindy saw her dad give back to the local community by working with the rescue squad and being a police officer. *"Giving back to our community was on both sides of the family. I also have worked for a local police department here in the New River Valley area for over 25 years, so you can say it runs in my blood."* In her job Cindy has the opportunity to do technical writing which she really enjoys.

"I enjoy doing the simple things in life. I love to craft, bake, sew and I also do woodworking and home improvements. I repurpose furniture and items to make them new again or changing a room to make it look totally different. I am so glad that I learned to sew from my grandmothers so that I can make things that will be around in the future for people to enjoy. I am grateful that I was able to spend time with my grandfather to observe of his woodworking skills. I don't have a lot of the skill but I know he would be proud."

Cindy continues to inspire as she provides teaching life skills to youth and to women; showing how to be resilient in their life. Her goal is to continue writing and speak to community organizations and schools. To contact Cindy visit her on the web at www.CindyLea.com.

Contact Cindy
- Website: www.CindyLea.com
- Email: CindyLeaWriter@gmail.com

TAKING ON WATER
by Dave Frett

TAKING ON WATER

"And behold, there arose a great storm on the sea, so that the boat was being covered with the waves;" - Matthew 8:24

The very famous author, J.K. Rowling, of the incredibly popular and successful Harry Potter series is known for having said, *"Rock bottom became the solid foundation on which I rebuilt my life."* Many people dread hitting the rocks of life, for they can be perilous and uncertain times. Even more destructive than hitting the rocks of life is hitting rock bottom. When a ship is entering an inlet, with rocks on both sides of the strait, it is imperative that the compass is accurate, and the rudder is straight, for this can be the difference between safety and destruction. Unfortunately, regardless of how much effort may be extended, there will be times in our lives when either the bottom truly falls out or we simply feel as if it has; either way we experience the harshness of being smashed around, struggling to find a piece of driftwood to hold onto just to keep from drowning in the cold undertow, while we wait for the rescue party to be dispatched.

The year was 2012 and as a family, we were about to undertake the largest change our family had yet to journey. After nearly four years of continuing education, thousands of hours of prayers, endless employment applications and the heavy hand of God's leading upon our lives, the time had finally come – God had opened the door for service at Liberty University. Our family would be selling our home, packing all our belongings, leaving all the family and friends we had ever known and moving over 400 miles away to Lynchburg, Virginia. In the midst of all the busy activities of this season in life, and as we were striving to follow and obey God's leading in our lives, we would come to find out how the attacks of the wicked one would be increased in an attempt to discourage and prevent us from following the

Lord's leading.

On Friday, March 16, 2012, simply one week before I was scheduled to move, we found ourselves in the hospital. Our youngest son, Luke, only five years old, had begun experiencing seizures and was diagnosed with epilepsy. At the same time, our health coverage was set to expire that exact weekend, seeing I had recently left my previous company after nearly 13 years of service. The uncertainty, the anxiety, and the fears of what lay before us assaulted our minds and souls. How could this be happening to us? I mean, we were leaving everything we knew to follow God's leading and obey His will for our lives. What would become of our little boy and this disease we knew little about? How would he be treated and how would we possibly afford the costs associated with it? How would I focus on a new job, find a new home for our family to live in and make all the transitions that come along with such a life change while my wife and boys remained in New Jersey to finish the school year and wrap up all that's required with moving? These are the real and amplified questions and fears that so often run through the minds of parents and individuals alike that are faced with external situations in which there is no control.

These are the moments when we feel out of control; as if our lifeboat is taking on water and we have no way to stop the sinking.

While as believers we know we are not immune to the attacks of Satan, we often forget how real and vicious the attacks can be and how frequent the onslaught can come; in fact, we walk around with a literal bulls-eye on our backs. I Peter 5:8 tells us, *"Stay alert! Watch out for your great enemy, the devil. He prowls around like a roaring lion, looking for someone to devour."* On the other hand, it has been expressed, *"In the greatness of our troubles there may often be space for the greater display of the goodness of God."*

Author and financial guru, Dave Ramsey, once wrote, *"Hitting bottom and hitting it hard was the worst thing that ever happened to me and the best thing that ever happened to me."* How many people do you know who would describe hitting rock bottom as the best and worst possible scenario in their life? Not many I would imagine. However, sometimes what is required is for us to be made so low, even prostrate, with no place to go but to look up and cry out for help. When pondering this thought I find it encouraging how Kirk Franklin noted, *"God may allow us at times to hit rock bottom, to show us He's the rock…at the bottom."*

As unnerving and intimidating as this situation with our son left us, it was only but another block in the building process of our lives. Were we willing to trust God? Were we willing to obey and follow in the tough times as well as the bountiful? What would this experience have to say regarding our faith? Was it truly faith in God or was it faith based upon circumstances?

Over the following four years, God has taught us the importance of leaning on Him and Him alone. Corrie ten Boom, an infamous figure during the Second World War under the persecution of Hitler and the Nazi regime, once wrote, *"You may never know that JESUS is all you need, until JESUS is all you have."* While having been raised in a Christian home; while having placed my faith and trust in Christ as my personal Savior while still a boy; and while having known about all the miracles Christ performed during His ministry on earth – now was the time to decide whether it would be merely theoretical understanding or whether it would be practical application.

When you are the person in the sinking boat (either real or perceived) is when your faith is truly tested.

There is no longer an opportunity for academics or to rely upon another's faith. The time comes that faith can't be simply rhetoric but factual. Growing up I spent many a day out on the water; whether fishing, clamming, or simply joy riding. As with any large amount of time spent, some days and trips provided beautiful sunny skies while others were masked in dark skies and turbulent waters. During those rough sea days, many a wave would break over the bow leaving the boat to take on water in need of running the bilge to relieve and remove. Some days were even so rough that in addition to the bilge system, I can recall having to manually fill and dispose of said waters with a bucket. As difficult and tedious as it was to have to gather water in such a manner, the fact that one had a hard time holding their footing made for an even more laborious task.

Here the comparison can be made about being on the rough seas in one's boat attempting to self-bail the water of one's life, as then the difficulties, challenges, and struggles come along that we attempt to resolve in our own strength and might. Even in the physical realm of the tangible boat and seas, one cannot bail and drive simultaneously. In order to get out of the trouble and treacherous waves, there must be at least two crewmen. There is no difference in our spiritual walk.

As a boy on the boat during these times, it was my duty to bail the water while my Dad maneuvered the seas. Today, as an adult – a husband, father, son, brother, uncle, friend, and most of all, Christ-follower – I need to stop presuming and acting as if I have the ability to remove myself from the threatening obstacles and incidences of life. In fact, I need to relinquish the reins of my life; I need to stop trying to bail my boat and drive; and I need to give it over to God - trusting Him, as I did my Dad, to guide me out of the storms and to safe ground.

I would venture to say that no one enjoys getting knocked down. Quite the contrary, we attempt to do whatever we can to avoid such situations. However, when it happens we seem to run around like Chicken Little, despairing and crying, *"The sky is falling. The sky is falling!"* No one enjoys bottoming out and certainly no one enjoys having their entire world turned upside down; however, having the knowledge that we have a support staff, a Captain and our Protector, in God Himself, can and should make all the difference.

We can be reminded in these words. *"We are hard pressed on every side, but not crushed; perplexed, but not in despair; persecuted, but not abandoned; struck down, but not destroyed. We always carry around in our body the death of Jesus, so that the life of Jesus may also be revealed in our body."* - II Corinthians 4:8-10

In Corinthians, the Apostle Paul went on to encourage the people that while they would face trials and conflicts, they also had the promise that God would never abandon them.

What do we do when we get knocked down?

Do we remain downtrodden and destitute or do we rise again, pressing on and overcoming? If we do attempt to rise again, do we attempt this on our own or do we look to another's strength? James wrote in Hebrews 13:5, God has said, *"Never will I leave you; never will I forsake you."* Despite the circumstances that one may find himself in, despite how fast your boat seems to be taking on water, and despite what storms you must go through in life - God is ALWAYS there!

Looking back to that emotionally charged and frightening time and event, God's hand has been evident in all segments of our family's life. Not only has He continued leading and providing for our family but He has blessed in immeasurable ways. While Satan has attempted time and time again to discourage and prevent God's unfolding will in our lives, as we have continued to obey and follow Him, He remains faithful, unwavering, and immovable in our lives. As we are now four plus years from this particular hospital stay, I can say truthfully and assuredly that God has healed our son completely. Luke no longer has to be medicated and no longer suffers from seizures. God, the Great Physician, has emptied the waters from the boat, restored the boat's structural integrity and placed us on a course storm-free and headed into the beautiful scenery of a setting sun on the horizon.

Will there be other turbulent waters and times ahead? Most certainly. As long as believers are willing to trust, obey, and follow Christ in all aspects of life, the enemy will persist in his attacks. He will not give up and he will not back down. That's the downside. The upside is that Christ is stronger and will always provide a way to overcome. Whether it was David who faced down a lion and a bear in preparation for his encounter with a giant or whether it was Daniel who chose to obey God rather than an irate king at the expense of being thrown to lions, whatever you may be confronting today, God is always strong enough to provide the rescue. He may never be early but He is always on time. The same promise found in Deuteronomy 20:4 is the same promise for you! *"For the Lord your God is the one who goes with you to fight for you against your enemies to give you victory."*

Many of us critique our lives based on how long we remain on top, how seldom we encounter problems and the degree of our struggles, or how high we fly. We become discouraged and even begin to rethink the value of our lives or the success of it when the bottom begins to fall out, whether by intentional fault or unintentional mishap. However if truth be told, just as George S. Patton once remarked, *"Success is how high you bounce when you hit bottom"*, the positioning of one's life or the highs and lows should never be the determining component of its effectiveness.

Life can be smooth and then boom. . .the attack comes!

We may begin questioning, *"Have I done something wrong? Why has this happened?"* In the Bible it says the enemy is out to destroy us; and while he desires to inflict pain and heartache, just know that God intends to use the experience to strengthen our faith, to cause us to seek His face, and to remind us He is our all in all.

Dr. Jerry Falwell Sr. used to say, *"Every believer is either coming out of a trial, in the midst of a trial or about to go into a trial."* Regardless whether an individual faces the prospective onset of rocky terrain or that the breaker has crushed you in splinters, what is most important is whether one stays down or gets back up. Do you rebuild the boat and cast a line or do you tie up in the harbor fearful to launch out for threat of more rocks? Do you allow God to teach you valuable lessons in those moments or will you as Job's wife encouraged him, *"Curse God and die."* As Muhammad Ali once trumpeted, *"Only a man who knows what it is like to be defeated can reach down to the bottom of his soul and come up with the extra ounce of power it takes to win…"*

Resilience is not found in one's own strength, understanding, or perseverance; instead true resilience is found in following Jesus' command. In Luke 9:23 He said, *"Whoever wants to be my disciple must deny themselves and take up their cross daily and follow me."* For the man or woman who neglects daily submission to Christ and the suffrage of His cross, but would rather attempt life in his own stead, the prospect of becoming an obedient follower and thus an overcomer with regard to life's battles will go unlearned and unachieved. When a man learns that the only weight he needs to bear is the cross of Christ, it is then that his life is freed and the burden is lifted. Jesus makes the promise when he tells us, *"For my yoke is easy and my burden is light."* – Mathew 11:30.

Today live as if you believe you're on the winning side.

Being a follower of Christ doesn't mean life will be easy; it does however reverberate that the world is at odds against us, for Jesus said in John 15:18, *"If the world hates you, keep in mind that it hated me first."* However, also keep in mind that we have resilience in our nature that is instilled by the living, Holy God who spared nothing to redeem us but gave everything. Jesus Himself reminded us in John 16:33, *"I have told you these things, so that in me you may have peace. In this world you will have trouble. But take heart! I have overcome the world."* Will you choose to live today as an overcomer or will you simply live overcome by the world?

Strategies for Building Your Resilience

Ask yourself these questions to gain insight:

1. Realizing everyone WILL experience hardships, what are you struggling with today? – I Peter 4:12

_____
_____
_____

2. Every one of us will get knocked down at some point; however, the blessing we have is that we don't need to stay down – I Peter 5:10. How have you learned to become resilient and climb up out of the pit you've fallen in to?

_____
_____
_____

3. Personal strength and resilience is foundational to life's success; however, sometimes regardless how resilient one may be, we need someone else's help.

Who has been there to lend a hand and teach you what resilience means in your darkest hours? Have you considered prayer? – I Corinthians 10:13

_____
_____
_____

4. Challenges, struggles, and trials are used to strengthen one's life. It has often been quoted, *"Whatever doesn't kill us makes us stronger"*. Do you consider what the lesson is that may need to be learned when going through the valley? What are some lessons that you have learned through the fire? – James 1:2-8

_____
_____
_____

5. The lesson and trait of resilience prepares us for life. Resilience aids perseverance in life and strengthens us, but as strong as resilience makes us, it also softens us - it softens us to empathize with and aid others. How has you experience allowed you to encourage others facing the same or similar times? – Acts 14:22

_____
_____
_____

About Dave Frett

Dave is a husband, father, author, but most of all, disciple of Christ. He was raised in a Christian home and accepted Christ as my personal Savior at the young age of 6 years old. Over the course of his life, he has experienced highs and lows just as any other believer. However, through it all, God has never given up on him.

In 1989 he went to college at Liberty University where he started as a ministry major. Due to experiences, both internal and external, he left college after two years. After returning home and beginning a career in retail management, he met his better half and soon married her. Almost three years after marrying Lindsey, God blessed them with their first, of ultimately four, sons. Dave began moving through and advancing within his field – however never feeling completely fulfilled.

After having been away from school for nearly 15 years God opened an opportunity for him to go back to school. He graduated Liberty University with a Bachelor's of Science in Business Management. Standing on the field at graduation he recall telling his family how he felt God calling him to serve Him there, so they started praying, pursuing, and continuing his Graduate education. After almost 4 years in this pursuit and wondering if it was ever going to happen, Dave received a call from Liberty University; after a few interviews, he was offered a position.

Now his family would once again step out by faith, moving over 400 miles from our families and friends, and starting over. It was quite a challenge and struggle, both emotionally, physical, spiritually, and financially. But God continued to provide. Dave graduated from Liberty with a Master's in Business Administration with a specialization in Leadership. Roughly two years into his tenure at Liberty University he began writing. The dream of writing had been placed on his heart years earlier but he never knew how that would occur or what it would look like. To be honest, he was always discouraged by the negativity on Facebook so he felt led to provide positive, God-driven content – which led him to begin writing devotionals. Over the last few years God has taught him much, in his own spiritual walk and in how to be an author. Dave has several books currently in production and is speaking on how to be strong in Faith. If you would like to talk with Dave or plan a workshop for his teachings please follow his Battlestrong Ministries group on Facebook, reach out to him at 609-709-4967 or visit his website at www.BattlestrongMinistries.com.

Contact Dave
- Website: www.BattlestrongMinistries.com
- Facebook: facebook.com/TheBattleIsReal
- Phone: 609-709-4967

THE IDENTITY OF RESILIENCE
by Dawn Briggs

THE IDENTITY OF RESILIENCE

"Resilience is accepting your new reality, even if it's less good than the one you had before. You can fight it, you can do nothing but scream about what you've lost, or you can accept that and try to put together something that's good." - Elizabeth Edwards

For those of us who remember John Edwards, a former presidential candidate and golden boy, the life of his wife, Elizabeth was less than easy. The death of a child, the diagnosis of breast cancer, the humiliation of her husband's affair and love child in the public eye, and the recurrence of her breast cancer leading to her early death made Mrs. Edwards one of my personal heroes. The grace and courage she showed in her last days gave her children permission to accept things life throws at them as building materials to construct a life well lived. Like any other skill, we need to practice acceptance and choose to be resilient. It takes believing in a power greater than ourselves to be faithful in meeting our needs so we can fulfill our divine purpose.

The strength in studying real stories of not just those that survive but thrive in the face of life challenges brings me the knowledge that I am not alone. The other stories in this book show ordinary people doing extraordinary things through life's challenges. Although for an average person, starting life from a less than perfect place can be a challenge. Life becomes the process of finding our destiny. It is in true acceptance that we are able to let go and move on.

Let me tell you a secret.

We live in a fallen world where no one among us is born into perfection; have parents that have it all together, or a marriage that stays together without a lot of work. No one has perfect children, or perfect health, every moment in life.

Born to a 24-year-old father and a 21-year-old mother who died just days after my birth, my identity became *"the little girl whose mother died when she was born."* It was my banner, my tattoo, my label for my early years of life. My dad's family – my beloved grandparents Caz and Arma, and my aunt Irene cared for me. I was loved and treasured. Monday through Friday became my favorite days of the week because I was home and my life was celebrated. The weekends however with my biological mother's family were filled with abuse of every kind and turmoil. The day of my birth was not celebrated with that family but rather became the anniversary of death.

Three years later my father married the woman who would be the great love of his life, the woman who would complete him, my wonderful mom, Nola. A larger than life Italian family of great fun, good food, and family members that loved each other, she had a little mother, grandma Sylvia who used to get up early morning on holidays and cook for hours. How I adored watching her move so easily making food that her family would spend hours enjoying with lots of conversation and lots of dishes to wash. You felt like you were part of something bigger than yourself. I love my mom. Through her, there would be friendship, acceptance, and my three brothers, David, Michael, and Joseph. Each of my brothers has had challenges they have had to work in order to craft amazing lives with their families. And this day mom and I rarely go 24 hours without speaking and still are friends after 60 years of life together. Things weren't always easy, but we made it out the other side with a shared love of my father. One of the most precious memories of my life will always be when I was standing next to my dad's casket several years ago and my mom came up next to me as we said goodbye together.

Over the next 30 years, two failed marriages, physical and emotional abuse, and cancer made every dream for my life end up on the trash heap except for one. In 1989 I met the little girl who would become my daughter, Melissa. At age five she had been through every abuse a person could suffer. I knew she needed a family and so did I. Together we faced the scars of our lives making it through one day at a time by the grace of God. And we are still learning. Born drug addicted and let down by our social service system she was alone in this world, or so we thought. Today we know that there are four other living siblings who share in the resilient gene, who I have contact with through Melissa. She is not alone and is my hero when it comes to resilience. She always finds the good in others without letting go of her own sense of self.

Sixteen years ago when I believed my life was all but finished and I was ready to live out my days with my daughter and my family, something happened to set me on my path. I met a man a friend…a single dad…a confidant who saw in me what I did not see in myself. He was loving, caring and focused with a serving heart like no other. Dave and I have been building our life together ever since. Now with sharing three grown children, nine grandchildren, and a life filled with laughter, animals, challenges, grief, joy, and passion. We face the world together head on walking hand in hand with God. All I ever wanted to be was a wife and mother. My heart is full to overflowing. How many of us take a step back and view our life as a tapestry? I'm sure you have heard it said that when we are living all we see are knots, loops, frayed edges, and colors of our lives. These are the threads of business, efforts, parenting, holding on to our sense of self, and the activities of day-to-day living. We don't see the big picture we are weaving in life. But our awesome creator looks from above and sees what we have created from the bits of threads and experiences in our journey that creates the story of our life. It is good.

If anyone told me what we would experience in those sixteen years I would have said, *"Stop the world…I want to get off!"* Two weeks before the wedding my beloved husband lost his job. We had three kids ages 14, 16, and 17 who were all getting into cars and looking at college. I was also diagnosed with fibromyalgia and rheumatoid arthritis, and heart issues. I needed to take 14 pills a day and became diabetic. As a result, I went blind in my right eye after five eye surgeries. I moved away from the only family I knew for my husband's new job in Colorado. I lost a job I dearly loved due to my health. In this season I also lost my husband's dad, experienced the death of my dad, and lost seven cats and one dog. And the list goes on just as life does.

But what did we gain?

We were able to appreciate the opportunity of steady work. I was able to work with small businesses needing help in administrative services that were on a tight budget. I also gained so many friends and supporters. These opportunities alowed me to travel to places like Seattle, Phoenix, Florida, California, Oregon, and Canada. I have gained an awareness of having children that are strong and resilient. They are raising wonderful and loving human beings that are learning these gifts of life. Our daughter Liz is a single mom. She is a labor and delivery nurse raising her children, Zack, Troy, and Audrey. She recently moved to Colorado from Arizona, and they light up our lives!

David and Renee left Colorado for Florida where they are building a real estate business and enjoying raising their sons, William and Jackson. They share a passion for Winston-Cup Racing. Melissa's children Steven, Khymberlei, Jasmyn, and Armonte, who live in Illinois, are never very far from our thoughts. We get back to

Illinois as often as we can to be with them and share our heart. They have come a long way in showing us a glimmer of the next generation of resilient and loving people.

A big element of resilience is how you decide to look at things.

I had an aunt who used to refer to the lot I had in life as a *"crap sandwich!"* She looked at the glass as not having anything in it at all, much less than half empty. Whether you are living life with a paper cup or cut crystal, have Kool-Aid or fine wine, live in a mansion or subsidized apartment, clothes from a designer showroom or resale shop, there are challenges and issues in life. What we choose to do with those challenges is what makes us human and defines our character. Today can you look at each challenge and say to yourself, *"What can I do today that will turn this into a win-win? What gifts do I have that can be used for the betterment of another? In what way can I build up instead of tear down?"* Each of us is responsible for playing the hand we have been dealt. Whether you decide you will or you won't, you are correct.

As I am writing this, I am facing two shoulder replacements due to the damage from rheumatoid arthritis. Is it a crap sandwich or just life? Should I sit and stew in the pain and be a victim or be grateful for hearing the laughter in my granddaughter's voice when she holds her baby kitten. The choice is fully mine. I could shout and complain (and there are days I do).

I am resilient, not a saint.

There are always those better off or worse off than me. If you haven't figured it out by now, resilience is not the absence of challenges affecting your life. It is finding that life is still purposeful through the challenges. Until they slam the lid or light the match on this tired body, finding the strength to put one foot in front of the other is a choice...like the choice to love or the choice to quit.

Resilience is not a *"pick yourself up by the bootstraps"* or *"fake it till you make it"* mindset. It is allowing yourself to be wounded while not lingering too long. It's reaching out for the hands that are sent to help you along the way. It's relying on a power greater than yourself to guide your steps towards the fulfillment of your place in this world. And then, resilience is sharing what you have been so freely given to help others who for that moment in time can only be helped by you. For me it was church family members, my best friend of several decades, Leslie and her mom, Marilyn and brother Kurt who are always there as a second family, and my cancer survivor family like Marla who I met on Facebook and who introduced me to Tricia, which led to being a part of this book. You never know when you meet someone how you will become a part of the fabric of their lives or them in yours.

It is said that the two most important days in your life are the day you were born and the day you know why. If you have never thought about your gifts, take a moment and reflect on what they might be. For me, I am a natural connector. In business networking, it has been my joy to connect professionals who deserve to know each other. I never know when I meet someone how they can be blessed by knowing who I know. And no matter how successful a day I may have, it's never a complete success until I have made a connection between two people. Early on in my career, this skill made it possible to connect husbands and wives, employers and employees, power partners and potential clients. And always it is my greatest joy to connect a friend or family member to my Lord and Savior, Jesus. I am humbled any time the God of the universe takes the time to introduce me to someone for a moment of prayer, a hug, or just a moment where He is present. That is real resilience.

Personal note from Tricia: At the editing of this story, Dawn came through her shoulder surgery but experienced a traumatic brain injury in a fall and has been in extensive rehab due to the body injury in her fall. She lost her eye sight in both eyes yet she is a warrior standing resilient and giving it to God. I am proud to call Dawn my friend as her loving heart and perseverance is a remarkable quality to experience in action. Due to her experience in the fall and being in rehab with severe issues, she has dedicated her life work to help be a voice for those in nursing home, rehab care, or who are alone with no care so they get the physical and spiritual help they need.

Strategies for Building Your Resilience

1. What three things today can you be aware of or grateful for, in spite of challenges you are facing?

_____
_____
_____

"Happiness is not inherently free of hardship or worry: it's a level of positive awareness and understanding we exhibit throughout and often despite the many challenges life bestows upon us. Happiness is, in other words, resilience." - Joseph Rain

2. Who is the person you are meant to be? Take some time and drown out all the voices surrounding your answer. You and only you guided by a loving God of your understanding can answer that question. There is a still small voice inside that must be heard. Who are you meant to be?

_____

_____

_____

"Stop messin' around. Be the person you are meant to be. Remember that somewhere someone is rooting for you to succeed! Don't worry about the others. They're too busy riding coattails, being unhappy, and making excuses as to why they gave up on their own dreams. You've got this. And if today you were wondering if you could do it? Consider this your pep talk."
- Dawn Garcia

3. From where does your light source come? Seek the light and list opportunities for brightness in your own darkness. Who are those that are cheering you on? This can change over time. Be aware today of those shining light on your journey and appreciate the light. Be aware of false light. In whose lives are you shining light today? Pick three and send a note, make a call, reach out in love expecting nothing in return.

_____

_____

_____

"We are in this together. None of us truly walk in isolation, even when we cannot sense the presence of another for miles upon miles. Even in the worst of our desolation. Even during our coldest 3am breakdown. Even when we shut out the world and spin in circles until we collapse. Even then the light still gets in. Even then the heart still opens and reaches, tendrils of hope curling and bending toward slivers of light.

Upward, outward, in all directions – seeking light at all cost. One way or another, we all grow toward the light." - Jeanette LeBlanc

About Dawn Briggs

Dawn Briggs, a transplant from Illinois to Parker, Colorado is a woman in her early 60's who has experienced God's grace in her life through loss, challenges, abuse, health issues, and great love. A mother of an adopted daughter Melissa who is resilient in her own right, stepmom to David and Elizabeth who continue to surprise her through their resilience to life's challenges and grandmother of nine she is walking through this journey of life with her beloved husband, Dave.

They have been married for 15 years and share a life of passion for grandchildren, animal rescue, and laughter. Helping small business owners through effective customer relations, and strong business ties through ne working in her company B.R.A.V.O. (Business Relationships Adding Value to Others) keeps Dawn busy even though she has now been given the vision to rename B.R.A.V.O. to Building Resilience Adding Value to Others.

What is interesting is that through the process of writing in this project and experiencing major health issues her calling has been revealed. Her church and others have come forward to help her minister and teach resilience to those who have been disabled, abandoned, or in situations where they may not be able to speak their needs. The gift in the storm has shown Dawn that her higher calling that God has set her on is to bring love into the darkness. Being blind and on a healing journey, she now sees things clearer than ever before.

To inquire about Dawn speaking, teaching or sharing her message of hope and resilience please email Dawn at Dawnderful@aol.com.

Contact Dawn
- Website: www.CLPLI.com/dawn_briggs
- Email: Dawnderful@aol.com

THE FUEL OF A PURPOSED LIFE
by Coni Meyers

THE FUEL OF A PURPOSED LIFE

Can you imagine going through childhood looking different than everyone around you? Can you imagine not having a mom that cared about you and was actually prejudice against you? This story is one of extraordinary resilience.

I would like to introduce you to Ginny, whom I met and interviewed at a recent retreat that I held. Ginny grew up looking different from her family members and her childhood friends. You see, Ginny was adopted as an infant from Korea during the Korean War. She, along with her three siblings were taken to an orphanage because her mother could no longer afford to care for them. Once there, a young American soldier saw Ginny while visiting the orphanage to hand out food, clothing and blankets. He and his wife, at home in Lisbon, Iowa, had already adopted two other children. But this young man wanted to make room back home for this three-month old baby girl. So he called his wife and she agreed to adopt this infant. In short order, Ginny became the first Asian in Lisbon, Iowa. This was in the early 1950's so she was probably the only Asian within 100 miles of Lisbon.

Ginny excelled in school. As an 'A' student who involved herself in many school activities, her teachers adored her. However, the same cannot be said of many of her schoolmates who only saw her as 'different' and who did their best to cause her to feel different. Fortunately, Ginny found comfort in her adoring father. She was definitely a *"daddy's girl"*. Unfortunately, when Ginny was only nine years old her life got turned upside down. Her father died! She soon realized that her mother was less than thrilled with having a Korean child in her home.

No matter how hard she tried to be loved or accepted it never happened. Her mom was actually prejudiced. Of course, this attitude was morphed into Ginny's siblings and she ended up with no relationship with anyone in her adopted family. She soon felt completely isolated and alone like a stranger among those that should have been her closest emotional ties.

Ginny was determined and committed to creating a good life.

The more that life set her back the harder she forged ahead. She went on to graduate from college with honors. She found the love of her life whom she married and they had two beautiful children. Ginny carved a wonderful life for herself, rich in family love and friends in the gorgeous artsy village of Ojai, California.

Ginny's next challenge came on the day she received a letter from her adopting agency. It stated that her biological family was looking for her. Her birth mother was dying and they wanted all of them to reunite as a family before that happened. What a shock! She had grown up being told that her Korean family was all dead! She felt that there had been a serious mistake and called them to say so. When the agency provided Ginny with a picture of a baby with a woman that matched closely with the one Ginny had in her possession she was distraught and confused. Certain that a visit to Korea would be necessary, she told her husband that she wanted to go alone because she didn't know what to expect.

Ginny made it to Korea in time to meet the woman everyone else called mom. When she walked into the hospital room her mother gasped and said, *"You're so DARK"*; a very unattractive look among Koreans in their country. Ginny lived in Southern California and had a suntan so she was much darker than any of her biological family. Having traveled halfway around the world to meet her first family for the first time, Ginny was embarrassed and wounded. She didn't know what to say or do. She was numb and confused and now felt rejected by her biological mom as well her adoptive mom.

When Ginny told me her story I was moved by her inner strength and resilience.

She had bridged and crossed the chasms in both families. She had battled the ridicule in school, and absorbed the loss of her father. Her strong, resilient inner spirit was evidenced by the lovely life she created for herself. These events she spoke of I refer to as crystalline moments or CM for short. Crystalline means sparkling or clear, so they are moments of clarity. Ginny had many of these moments. The resilient way she handled these sad discoveries moved her forward...each step fueling her for the future.

Like most of us, Ginny had experienced many life altering been moments. She stepped forward like a baseball player at bat, not knowing if she would strike out or hit a home run. By stepping into oncoming missiles, she had the incredible opportunity of reconnecting with her heritage. Her children would have the same experience as well, embracing her Korean family of aunts and uncles who looked much like them and their mother. We all have events in our lives that either propel us forward or paralyze us. Ginny could have held onto her fear of the unknown about her Korean family, but the resilience developed over the years propelled her to accept this new challenge.

I too have been knocked down repeatedly and have had to start over numerous times.

With resilience I pushed through to the other side, stepped up to the plate with determination and persistence. In preparation for writing this chapter, I asked people what resilience means to them. What was their answer? Starting over, overcoming, bouncing back, getting up again, pushing through, and 'stepping up' to the plate, determination and persistence. We all have times in our lives when we face challenges and we must decide what we are going to do. How are we going to move forward or are we going to be paralyzed and stay stuck.

Have you had a major event in your life that leaves you feeling paralyzed? Do you feel you can't move forward? What is the source of your failing to move on? How you react reveals your level of resilience, among other things. The opposite of moving forward is moving backward or being paralyzed, stuck, or trapped.

I'm not saying this boastfully, but I have learned that I am very resilient and the people I most admire have also developed this important attribute. The direct result of the amazing stories of resilience I heard from family, friends, and acquaintances became my first best seller, *"Crystalline Moments"*. In my book I talked about how to find the opportunities that are created by each of these moments. Resilience is the fuel that propels people forward into those opportunities.

Each of the people in my book, *"Crystalline Moments"*, share of their own crystalline moment which created opportunities that led to their living a life they love. It's the fire of resilience that moves us from where we were to where we are supposed to be. With determination and persistence, we advance from one step to the next step and so on. This fire of resilience propels us into the next opportunity resulting from our next CM. The more resilient we are the more forward we move and the less likely we'll become paralyzed or stuck.

Be committed is another facet of resilience.

Each of the fourteen individuals whose experiences I shared in my book showed commitment. They examined their crystalline moments, saw the opportunity and stepped into it. When you think of resilience, think of all those that you know who have overcome through commitment, determination, and persistence.

When Dale Carnegie was asked what it took for people to be resilient he said, *"Develop success from failures. Discouragement and failure are two of the surest stepping stones to success."* Resilience harnesses your inner strength to overcome serious setbacks. When lacking resilience, the tendency is to dwell on the 'problem', to run it around in your head over and over like a Ferris wheel, feeling victimized and overwhelmed. At this point, many turn to unhealthy ways of coping. You know them...sleep, booze, drugs, etc. If an infant learning to walk never got up when he fell he would never learn to walk. Learn to appreciate that each misstep or failure is a course correction. Certainly resilience will not make a problem go away, but it will give you the ability to see past them, find enjoyment in life and better handle stress. You learn to look for solutions and to implement those solutions.

When I was in my late twenties I was very successful in the insurance industry. I won 'Rookie of the Year' for Metropolitan Life Insurance. The next year I was made a sales manager. Of the fifty sales teams I took mine from forty ninth to third. In 1980, I was the only female sales manager in the western United States. There had been one other woman but was forced to quit due to a job related nervous breakdown. I too experienced similar harassment and pressure but was resilient enough to push my way through it.

The company created a grueling competition for the sales

managers. Seven days a week 12 hours a day wasn't enough. When accepting my award, I was handed a **man's** cardigan. I spoke with the regional manager and told him I wanted a **woman's** sweater. He said I would have to contact headquarters in New York. I did call the New York office and they refused to send a different sweater. I went back to the same regional manager, who had been sexually harassing me on a regular basis, and his advice was, *"Give it to your husband."* I told him, *"My husband didn't win this contest, I DID!"* Furious, I threw it at him and told him I quit.

I and the man who recruited me left Metropolitan Life and started a master general insurance agency. About this time a new life insurance policy called *"Universal Life"* came on the scene. I started reviewing my client list from Metropolitan and realized that this was a much better product for them. So I committed a big no-no and brought most of my clients on board with me. I eventually received a letter from Metropolitan's attorneys telling me to STOP. Now I 'step up to the plate' again and I returned the letter to my former regional manager and told him to leave me alone or he would find himself on the front page of the Los Angeles Times. He knew what I meant. State Farm had just lost a major lawsuit for discriminating against women.

Over the next few years, my partner and I built a very successful agency. Then he took to using crack cocaine. One day we had numerous agents into the office for training. He didn't show up until 7pm when most had already left for the day. He created an ugly scene. My fire kicked in. The next morning I went to the office and told my assistant that I was leaving the company. I packed and left. What I didn't realize is that my partner's signature was on the agreements for the contracts for the various products and not mine. I wanted contracts in my own name unfortunately I lost and he gained about $250,000 in my commissions. I was a naive and trusting 28 year old farm girl from Nebraska. I did come close to a nervous breakdown this time.

It was time for a course correction.

My best friend was moving to Portland, Oregon and asked me to come with her to gain some perspective. That's exactly what I did.

When I got off the plane in Portland it was as though I knew this is where I belonged. It was like walking into that perfect house, it just felt right. A crystalline moment led to an opportunity and my resilience paid off with big dividends. I was able to bounce back by creating a new life for myself that I hadn't thought possible. A few years later I sent a thank you letter to my former business partner. I didn't call these crystalline moments at that time but I did come to believe that things do happen for a positive reason. Resilience pushed me through those trying times and moved me toward the opportunities that became apparent. As Dale Carnegie stated, *"Failures and discouragement are the stepping stones of success we must accept and move forward in our journey."* We do so by resolving not to stop, to look for the opportunity that becomes available especially from our failures. Life may need only a small course correction or it may be a complete redirection of our steps.

Elizabeth Edwards says *"This is the life we have now, and the only way to find peace, the only way to be resilient when these landmines explode beneath your foundation, is first to accept that this is your new reality…our old lives no longer exist and the more we cling to the hope that they might come back, the more we set ourselves up for unending discontent."*

Once more I'll use my life as an example. When my husband

passed away five years ago I came to realize that I couldn't go back to the life I had been living. Professionally, I had owned four companies, two of which I took from a local market to the national stage. I believed that this was a successful life. Upon his death, I was forced to examine my life to see if I was living with purpose and really doing what I felt I was put on earth to do. Crystalline moments came flooding in along with the opportunities. I have since become a professional coach and speaker. I offer retreats for business and personal development as well as online workshops. My greatest joy is observing the resilient movement of my clients as they create the life they feel they were put on earth to live.

If today you have lost your forward motion and you feel stuck or trapped, examine what thoughts or events led you there. These are crystalline moments. Now visualize the life you want to have and look for the opportunities in each of these moments. Use your resilience, your fire, to power you into the steps that will take you there. If you feel you need to be more resilient examine what you think is holding you back then walk through the fear or sense of lack and your resilience will grow stronger each time.

Strategies for Building Your Resilience

1. Examine events from your past and how you moved forward.
_____
_____
_____

2. Are you stuck right now? What do you think needs to happen to get you moving forward in some way?

_____
_____
_____

3. Appreciate that these events or crystalline moments lead to new and better opportunities. Have you experience a shift; a crystalline moment in your life where you realized life needed to change? What was it?

_____
_____
_____

4. Next decide what step you must take to move you toward a designed life.

_____
_____
_____

5. Acknowledge that within you there is a small flame waiting to become a fire.

_____
_____
_____

6. If you feel you need to be more resilient work on how to overcome whatever is holding you back. What is holding you back? Be honest and let it flow. Is there a belief that you are holding on to that is sabotaging you?

_____
_____
_____

7. Become committed, determined, and persistent…RESILIENT.

About Coni Meyers

Coni Meyers has spent 35 years supporting individuals and businesses in their sales and marketing efforts. She has been a principal in 6 companies, of which two of them went from local markets to the national stage. She received the prestigious Life Mastery Consultant Certification, Certified Dream-builder Coach, and is a Certified John Maxwell Business and Leadership Coach.

Coni has 2 bestselling books. The first, *"Crystalline Moments"* is being read around the world showing people how to find opportunity in their own *"Crystalline Moments"*. The next book in the series is going to be on Crystalline Moments in Adoptions. She has 6 additional titles in this series. *"The Success Chronicles"* her second book addresses how to have true success in your life and business. Coni's passion has helped 1000's step into the lives they would love both personally and professionally. She does so through her speaking, coaching, training, online classes, workshops, and retreats.

Coni founded CKM - Coaching, Knowledge & Marketing Solutions with the goal in mind of creating unique programs that will change people's lives. She has just completed 2 new offerings. Her Crystalline Moment Success Movement and her signature program called SOLVE - The Solution for Your Life and Business. *"Create true SUCCESS by discovering your Crystalline Moment OPPORTUNITES provided by great LEADERSHIP, VISION and ENGAGEMENT".*

Coni's personal passions are wine, cooking, art, and jazz. She has created a life she loves that extends way beyond the US borders and includes her children, family, and friends around the world. She truly loves the life she is living and wants to help others to do the same. To reach Coni Meyers visit her website at www.CrystallineMoments.com.

Contact Coni
- Website: www.CrystallineMoments.com
- Email: Coni@ConiMeyers.com
- Phone: 503-805-6621

AGAIN SPRING
by Mark Williams

AGAIN SPRING

"See, I am doing a new thing! Now it springs up; do you not perceive it? I am making a way in the desert and streams in the wasteland…I provide water in the desert and streams in the wasteland, to give drink to My people, My chosen, the people I formed for Myself that they may proclaim My praise." – Isaiah 43:19-21

Until recently, RESILIENCE has not been a word I connected with my identity. I never considered RESILIENCE a word that I would use to *"describe the rhythm of my life."* But, just like when you buy a new car–you see one just like yours everywhere, RESILIENCE could be my make, model, engine spec, color, and most outstanding asset for resale value.

In his 1828 dictionary, Noah Webster defined RESILIENCE as *"the act of leaping or springing back or rebounding, as in the resilience of a ball or of sound."* Literally, its Latin root means *"again spring"*.

Call it what you will, but, my wordsmith mind uses RESILIENCE as a new and different paradigm to shift my experiences into a life-giving perspective that no past or present amount of pain, discouragement, degradation, disillusionment, frustration, detouring, threat, arrogance, confusion, or waiting can overcome.

RESILIENCE is one of God's favorite words to speak about me. Because He says so, following every winter of my life, there is *"again spring."* Hear Him speak RESILIENCE about you.

1958-1969 RESILIENCE is…FIRST "DOWN"

In February 1958, snow fell on the house where my parents, two sisters, and grandparents lived, awaiting my arrival. By March, birth came, but not before my Mom and I were almost lost in its process. My aunt took care of me until Mom was home and able. Mom picked up where she left off–in less than a year, the household grew from four to six to seven. By June, my grandfather died. House hunting began. For the next four years, my Dad (now 44) was searching for himself at work, at church, at bowling, and at *"lost."* My Mom was the role of wife, mother, and daughter to mother-in-law, and like many, forgetting herself. We kids were growing somewhat obliviously. It was then I found the music in me. All of us were involved in the life of our church. Mom and her widowed best friend Anne were singing in the choir and Deacon dad, was helping Anne get over her grief.

One day, while Dad and I were on an errand, we stopped by at her house. I waited in the car for Dad. A while had passed by and they came to the door. They spoke a few more words, and kissed each other goodbye. Dad got in the car and drove us home. The whole time I sat quietly, feeling something was not right. At home, Dad asked me why I was so quiet, and I answered, *"I don't understand why you kissed Aunt Anne like you kiss Mom."* My simple question was an unexpected history-changing falling domino that changed our household forever. I experienced und served un-forgiveness as distance, disapproval, and devaluation. Our family business closed. Our church became uncomfortable.

God took over as my Father.

Not without pain, our new house was built. In 1963, we found a new church, and the road of family forgiveness formed before our feet. My mother led the way, never losing the song within her. I began life's journey to discover my identity and the place where I belong. I discovered the love of my Father. I *"agreed to be His precious child"* – created to make a difference in His world.

In the spring of 1966, my six weeks of measles-pneumonia-chicken pox was followed by my grandmother and uncle passing within one week. My third-grade year was over and we moved into a new smaller home. In a new way, I was finding me, again. This time, it was in the awkward cruelty of middle school. This winter was long DOWN.

Un-forgiveness assumes many forms. I felt its distance, disapproval, and devaluation on some level everywhere, except where I sought God's presence. I found God's presence…in my Dad doing ministry together, in my Mom's every choice, in my sisters' conversations, and in my church's belief in me. No matter where I was, I knew God was with me and it would be "again spring."

RESILIENCE KEY #1: As difficult as any DOWN may be, forgiveness will unexpectedly transform a dark paralyzing prison into a bright, powerful perspective.

1970-1981 RESILIENCE is SECOND…"UP"

UP is in the eye of the beholder. UP is as much of a decision as it is a direction as it is a destiny. UP is a reintroduction.

By Christmas 1970, we were moving back "UP the shore". UP meant returning to junior high friends without the benefit of shared middle school experiences. UP was reintroduction to people who had changed, me included. It was getting UP every morning to the fact that growing UP is not the same for everyone. Living UP to teenagers' expectations is impossible and their comments can be as painful as torn ligaments or as productive as micro-torn muscle. UP is not always seen, but it is always felt. UP requires energy exchange and has a variable threshold of pain. UP is as productive as you allow it to be.

Moving west to Pennsylvania was unexpectedly moving UP. I discovered that some relationships were for a season and others are for a lifetime. I discovered some investments are worth making and some people are only taking. I discovered only God's love lasts forever. I discovered some people like you because you are like them and some people don't like you because you are unlike them. I discovered some people enjoy the uniqueness differences make. Some high school and college friends were present to value me, some to challenge me, and some to galvanize me. UP is not all academic; UP means engaging relationships.

Looking back, I see that God places a holy dissatisfaction in us to reduce all tendencies to assume we have arrived at full stature and full maturity. God opened doors and I walked through them to walls that required climbing. They led UPward.

In US Army ROTC, they were tangible walls that tested both security and strength, mental walls that tested both strategy and wisdom, and soul walls that tested both character and resolve. I faced the question, *"What makes you think you can climb a wall?"* with action for the first time in my life. But, with that physical challenge completed, UP was not done with me yet. My call to ministry (not long after) sent shock waves through my soul.

Moving UP is often test upon test.

I left my ROTC commission with an honorable discharge only after witnesses testified on my behalf in a military hearing. Philippians 3:14 has never looked the same since that day.

My Dad's own occupational struggle took me on an *"internal integrity"* journey. What I saw first in industrial-organizational psychology led to developmental psychology then to God's clear call to ministry. I could-should-would not relive my father's *"lost self"*. After college graduation, God opened a youth ministry door in central New York. Disappointment and abandonment became the joyful passageway to discover my best friend. She was the wife God created for me. Yes, all who met her agreed, I would be marrying UP!

RESILIENCE KEY #2: Since UP is not a *"given"*, engaging relationships is required to rise. Engaging relationships requires having your eyes wide open to see the purpose beyond what's *"obvious"*.

1982-1993 RESILIENCE is THIRD…"STANDING"

Stand for something/someone or fall for anything/anyone. What was true 34 years ago is just as true today. STANDING always has its *why*. Falling always has its *why not*.

My wife and I chose one another to be 'The someone' to share our future, because in God's providence 'No one' else would do.

STANDING for something or for someone is a choice. It is a daily choice we make.

Finishing seminary required using my God-given mind, gifts, maturity, faith, and more. The challenges of each academic and field assignment prepared us for the new chapter of Bar Harbor. Before we arrived there, STANDING against came in two options. We demonstrated a new option: STANDING with one another in the presence and power of the Holy Spirit. The multiplying result I've come to know and expect is called heal and grow. It is amazing how people are drawn to people who are committed to one another. STANDING with people multiplies effectiveness, enjoyment, character, unity, appreciation, cooperation, creativity, productivity, and more. Its lessons never fade. You want to be together always, even when you used to be apart. This kind of standing has an impact and an influence that lasts a lifetime. Because of this, our family grew in RESILIENCE.

Our first call to *"the city"* brought us to Amesbury, Massachusetts, on the north shore of Boston. Our intention to stand with turned into STANDING against the works of the enemy. Our congregation was filled with suspicion, mistrust, and fear on the inside, all the while donning masks of *"We're fine. We're alright. Don't you know?"* Relationship addiction, substance abuse, passive aggressiveness, and fear of losing control make strange bedfellows. Similar things put Jesus on the cross, while friends stood by watching. Even staunch evangelical conservatives will set the Bible aside to defend disobedient friends in order not to lose them or face embarrassment again.

Patiently STANDING against the enemy opens new doors.

Pittsburgh was God's choice for our growing family. It was God's choice for a new church. For us, it also meant STANDING together alone in necessity. Starting everything out new can be exciting and hard work. Not everyone is cut out for all things new. Comfort is often found in a familiar zone. Relationships accelerate in this environment. Buckingham Palace guards know STANDING backwards and forward, inside and out. Sports teams move skillfully on their feet. Going from DOWN to UP and then to STANDING is the drink, the bread with the butter, and appetizer course of RESILIENCE. It is what you consume while preparing for the main course. It can be very good, but there is substantively more.

Our son and daughter were born in these years. They learned RESILIENCE watching us and with us. And we, were STANDING in RESILIENCE for them.

<u>RESILIENCE KEY #3:</u> STANDING is the visible manifestation of RESILIENCE within. If 'UP' says staying DOWN is not an option, 'STANDING' says UP was not accidental.

1994-2005 RESILIENCE is FOURTH…"FORWARD"

Backward for any length of time is rarely normal, if not 'down right' crazy. FORWARD has its moments, but FORWARD it must be. FORWARD is the future as living in the past does not make a new life.

FORWARD is direction.

It is certainly at its basis an implied choice. When our family moved from a three bedroom house in Amesbury with an attic, basement, and garage into a three bedroom apartment in Pittsburgh with a large freezer sized storage closet, it was at least an implied choice. It didn't always feel forward, but our growing children inspired FORWARD *direction*.

FORWARD was everything about what was possible, available, potentially scary, but positively fun anyway. It was blazing a trail similar to another, but never walked on before. At the beginning, FORWARD is (WestPoint) an adventure. Kids young and old love it. The old at heart would say, *"not so much"*. Everything FORWARD was *"all that and a bag of chips"*. That hasn't changed.

FORWARD is slow and stable.

"Are we there yet?" becomes an all too familiar phrase. Sometimes FORWARD must be inspiring, especially when progress or resources come to a halt. FORWARD reconstitutes itself as *"We fishin', because we ain't cuttin' bait!"* One good round of that version of FORWARD is all that's necessary, when it feels like you've

seen that side of the mountain before. An Old disabled church, a new challenging (CC) church, and a borrowed healthy (WR) church can all look strangely the same; producing the same set of choices that must be made to go FORWARD slow and stable. Moving FORWARD is a strange type of RESILIENCE, but genuine nonetheless. It can seems less fun, but it is discovered preferable when FORWARD is deceptively opposed.

FORWARD is tested.

The whole family feels the opposition, the pain, the frustration, and the pressure when things are a challenge. Even walking into a hot sandblast sounds like a great option. We know the winds will change–but when and which way? One crowd will say, *"Just how determined did you say you are to move FORWARD?... Did I hear you right?... You didn't actually plan to keep on moving FORWARD did you?"* Another crowd will say, *"We've come too far to stop now...We've lost the dead weight anyway...We're together and that's all that matters, isn't it?"*

When FORWARD is tested, you alone answer for you.

This season is critical. *"Again spring"* is decided here. It is bought here; galvanized here. Children choose not to grow up here. Adults are separated from immaturity here. Comfort is no longer the goal–it is instead enjoyed when the opportunity visits whether overnight or for an extended stay. You decide to grow up to go up with or without familiar companions, because you know with God you are never alone. By His design, spring comes again.

RESILIENCE KEY #4: The good old days looked better when you were younger. Now, they are just old. Tomorrow's better memories are created by looking and choosing and moving

FORWARD.

2006-2016 RESILIENCE IS FIFTH…"PERSEVERANCE"

Far too many people quit when PERSEVERANCE would be *"the priceless choice"* preceding manifestation of *"worth it all"* RESILIENCE. The Bible teaches PERSEVERANCE is rewarded with "the crown of life". The wise say everything worth working towards is gained from an uphill climb.

If FORWARD is peacefully predictable, PERSEVERANCE is *memorably motivating.*

COMPARE

"Remember when we were facing the right way and we didn't stop no matter what happened or didn't."
"
At least, we were moving in the right direction and didn't stop!"

WITH

"Who could possibly forget how so easily we could have quit, then suddenly everything we worked so hard for came to be!"

All we see now is amazing possibilities of what we can do with what started as determination to know God's great plan!"

What do you choose?

In the season of PERSEVERANCE, obstacles are turned into creative ideas that sometimes work and sometimes don't. But if you never try, you never discover how one creative idea that doesn't work leads to the one creative idea (once off the radar screen) that majestically takes flight! This sounds good, if not—poetically inspirational. But seriously, with every pitiful motive turned to every good intention, and for every good intention turned to something that has the potential to transform lives, you will settle for just FORWARD? Not I.

Once a toxic church and now a freed people…Once a Christ-centered business, and now a challenge completed…Once a distant dream of speaking and writing to now a legacy for making a lasting difference in the lives of many. Years of loving truth-telling, faithful relationship-building, mixed reviews receiving, resources invested, and opportunities expanding, the best efforts of giving and lives transforming—all prove PERSEVERANCE is worthwhile.

Spring is a season of new growth—slightly obvious. Extremely obvious is summer, a season of exponential growth. Yet, fall and winter make oftentimes overlooked contributions to growth. Most times people simply know about what gets most people's attention. Rarely do we hear anything about what happens inside a plant when summer has ended, and all the produce has been harvested as well as the flowers all picked. Just as rarely, do we hear anything about the changes that take place in soil when plowing, fertilizing and producing is *"for now"* done.

GROWTH never stops…RESILIENCE inherent is required! It is the never ceasing energy of life within us that makes what's next possible! Everything outside the seed-turned-plant makes what's inside come forth by God's design! Could that be true for me? Could that be true for you?

Every internal battle conquered is one down—Next!

Because my wife, my children, and my grandchildren are

watching…Because my parents, my sisters, and their families have waited…Because my friends and my cloud of witnesses have wondered it is FORWARD (once spring, now winter) that must turn into PERSEVERANCE– *"again spring!"*

<u>RESILIENCE KEY #5</u>: What will you make of all the resources available to you? Nothing is without perseverance. What LEGACY will YOU leave to the generations to come?

What will you do with the season you are in, so that the season to come will produce the results of RESILIENCE? This question is not meant to be condescending or terrifying. In the most compassionate way, it is meant to be challenging. If all of us experience challenges in life, and we do, then what makes the difference between those that GROW to make a difference and those who do not? I believe the answer is a choice to view the seasons of life through the perspective of RESILIENCE.

Whatever comes your way, you must know that it is the raw materials for the God-given purpose for which you were created. The laboratories of the world continue to discover amazing uses for the simplest of things. What about you? What do you have available for your creative use? What has taken you DOWN has the same power to take you UP–it's called rebounding.

What has brought you UP has the same power to make you STAND. What has made you STAND has the same power to propel you FORWARD. What has propelled you FORWARD has the same power to energize you to PERSEVERE!

Strategies for Building Your Resilience

1. What have you been tempted to quit/stop that you are willing now to do? How will you draw on God's life-giving power to complete?

_____
_____
_____

2. Who must you forgive and for what must you forgive them, in order to leave the dark paralyzing prison you're in and enter into a bright powerful perspective?

_____
_____
_____

3. Engaging relationships is required to rise up. Seeing beyond what's obvious requires eyes wide open. List those you've looked at externally that deserve closer attention. Who must receive more of your attention, and who less?

_____
_____
_____

4. If UP says staying down is not an option, for whom are you intentionally willing to stand for? What values or principles are you willing to intentionally stand for?

_____
_____
_____

List those who need to know you are intentionally with them.

_____
_____
_____

List those things you will intentionally prioritize going forward.

_____
_____
_____

How could your life change for the better by doing this?

_____
_____
_____

5. What memories must you downsize to make space for upgraded living?

_____
_____
_____

List daily thoughts you will replace to create a lifetime of reasons to celebrate.

_____
_____
_____

6. Separate the following into these categories. Map out in each section the resources and actions that would create a legacy you would profoundly and joyfully leave with your name on it.

Your Relationships:
_____
_____
_____

Your Experiences:
_____
_____
_____

Your Possessions:
_____
_____
_____

Your Strengths and Abilities:
_____
_____
_____

About Mark Williams

Because he deeply believes growth is grounded in God-given identity, Mark will tell you that he is a blessed son, brother, husband, and dad of two, father-in law of two, granddad of two and who knows how many more!

With over 30 years of senior pastor experience in Maine, Massachusetts, and Pennsylvania, his personal mission is to be an Ambassador of healing reconciliation, renewing vision, and growing hope. His work as a Growth Ambassador places him in the role of pastor, speaker, teacher, author, coach, mentor, and friend. In this season, he is learning to love the person he is yet *"becoming"*.

"Personally, one of my highest joys and accomplishments is found in watching people discover the healing reconciliation of whom and whose they are, the renewing vision of life they are created to live, and the growing hope their best days are still ahead!" To get in touch with Mark, please reach out at Mark@GrowingMaximizedLeaders.com and visit his website at www.GrowingMaximizedLeaders.com.

Contact Mark
- Website: www.GrowingMaximizedLeaders.com
- Email: Mark@GrowingMaximizedLeaders.com

GOD MIGHT WRECK YOUR DREAMS

by Betsy Ferguson

GOD MIGHT WRECK YOUR DREAMS

"So whenever plans fall by the wayside remember that God is simply saving you." - Dylan Crain

Go ahead, make a plan. I dare you. We are obsessed with making plans. We fill-up our life planners or Google calendars with appointments and meetings like it's our job. Our consensus is, 'if we aren't busy we aren't making money.' Go, go, go! Plan, plan, plan. But then the traffic jams happen. People don't show up or they walk out and all our plans are thrust into chaos. Proverbs 16:9 says that *"the heart of man plans his ways, but the Lord establishes his steps."* I was creating my dream job, dream team, and dream business. Everything I had been building over the last two to three years was to establish a successful, high volume, mega-agent expansion team in real estate. The business plan that seemed so right was actually all wrong.

I recently came out of a very painful season of my life. In some ways it seems the best way to describe it was a nightmare. People I had called friend, who I trusted, betrayed me. This was the first time in my life I had experienced girlfriends who I worked with betray and use me. It did not happen all at once. It came in waves over a period of time very similar to a storm in the Atlantic coming on shore; God stripping away the layers and taking away those I called *"friend"*. The reality was they were my joy stealers. I still love and care for each of them. I have forgiven them. A part of me even misses them. Strange to admit, I know. I miss what was or what I thought there was. I spent the majority of my time and days with my work team. I saw them more than I did my own family. The painfulness I have experienced through this season has been a process to move through. And one I will never forget.

I have the tendency to always look for the best in others. In my marriage my husband has titled me the *"optimist"*. I had my guard down for many years thinking I was invincible. Because of my ignorance I found myself being used and taken advantage of.

My business was growing massively. It was the natural snowball effect from years' worth of hard work and dedication. I was beginning to feel overwhelmed. I thought if I had someone to share the business load, it would allow for more balance with my family, for a real family vacation, and even lower my stress. I decided to approach an acquaintance about going into business with me. She was smart, had a good head on her and we shared the same religious beliefs. I thought that would be a good makeup to a solid foundation to go into business. I had admired her from afar for years. We knew a lot of the same people. We had attended the same local university and she was only a couple years ahead of me. She was great at what she did and there were many times we jived and rolled! At some point though, I will never know exactly at what point, she saw me as an opportunity for an easy way for her to come by money and a residual income. Of course at the time I didn't realize this. Again I look for the best in others which at times can cause me to miss signs that may be obvious to others. Within the first month of our partnership she had a terrible bicycling accident. She was hit by a granite truck at a four-way stop. After surgery she went through a 2-3 month recovery. Obviously this accident was completely out of her control, but I still shared 50% of all our earnings with her. I highly recommended we get some business policies into place for short term / long term disability as well as business overhead coverage so we would be prepared if something were to happen to her again or myself. I was surprised that she did not see this as a priority. Soon after being able to fully walk again she informed me she was pregnant. This was not an accident. It was planned. She told me so. We still didn't have the policies in place and I became very angry inside as I knew it was now too late to get her maternity leave covered. I didn't understand why she would willingly put financial strain on me and our business again. I chalked it up as ignorance on her part.

I showed kindness. It was her first baby. I knew my husband and I would be wanting a second child eventually so I decided to offer her what I hoped to take with my next child. 12 weeks of leave and take home 50% of the earnings. In hindsight I gave too much. The business partnership was out of alignment from day one but I couldn't see it at first and then once I did it was very difficult to admit.

I can see now it is important to be aware of give and take. You see there are givers and takers in this world. Beware of the takers in your life; the ones who only call or text when they need something. You will know a true friendship if it is balanced by give and take. My husband and I are naturally both givers. Whenever someone gives us a gift or does something for us that neither one of us expect, we have a difficult time accepting it. It feels weird. We are more likely to be on the giving end so to receive and actually accept a gift, from someone who isn't family, doesn't feel normal to us. I gave beyond what I should have in this business partnership. I made sacrifices I vow to never make again. I was rarely home and with my family. I missed out on the things that really mattered through this season. There was no balance in my life. I allowed myself to take on too much and a business partner who is truly a partner should not only acknowledge this but make changes to alleviate and balance out the work load. It was my very first business coach who coached me to see the light. She knew it long before I did that it wasn't truly a fifty percent partnership. She was patient with me though and over a six month period I came to see it for myself. The day I discovered the truth it hit me like a ton of bricks. Devastation, embarrassment, ignorance, and used; these were just some of the things I felt.

I was depleted, I had given everything. Even my health was at its worst.

Running through fast food drive thru's had become the norm because I didn't have the energy or the time to properly plan meals. My husband at the time was working an average 60 plus hours a week, six days a week. And he was the one who picked up the slack because my weeks were closer to 80 hours. He is my hero. He managed to maintain our home and keep a close relationship with our sweet daughter who really needed her mommy, but daddy would have to fill that during this season. I am grateful though it was my husband spending the bulk of the time with her and not a sitter. These are just some of the sacrifices that were made that weren't worth it. After finding out from my partner during her maternity leave she was moving out of the area but still wanted a percentage of residual income I knew it was time to do what I needed to do. I sat down and told her we needed to part ways. She felt entitled to a large payout. Because of this I had to hire myself an attorney to negotiate with hers. It was a painful and hard lesson. My dear, sweet, retired dad volunteered to let us borrow the money to make her go away. He didn't really have it himself but he could see the only other option would be to take a loan from a bank. It took nearly two months to negotiate the settlement but thankfully it was over.

I was in the middle of this painful pruning season thinking it was coming to an end, when in fact I was still gearing up for the next big storm. I claimed *"joy"* as one of my words for 2016. I wanted more joy in my life. Within a few short months while launching my own independent real estate brokerage we had massive turnover. More than half our people walked out. Ironic that God would allow the people I called *"friend"*, who were in fact my joy stealers, to continue to fall away from my life and business. He gave me exactly what I prayed for. It was just packaged very differently from what I had envisioned. God certainly does have a sense of humor.

When you are in the thick fog of a storm it is difficult, nearly impossible to see what God is doing; where it is headed.

I have always been a person of dominance and need to control things. When all this began unraveling in my life I quickly realized I couldn't stop it or take control over it. I had to exercise faith and trust in the unseen and unknown future. Challenging for me in that situation would be an understatement. I had never experienced so many people turning on me at once. I began to claim Nehemiah chapter 4. In this chapter it plays out that Sanballet ridiculed the Jews with insults and plotted trouble against them. Even still Nehemiah and his people pressed on with building the wall because that was the vision God had given him. And God took over the situation, protected Nehemiah and his people from the critics.

When you walk in the Spirit and the vision the Spirit God has given you, know that you will have critics.

A tool to use to know if the vision you heard was truly from God ask yourself, *"Did I really hear from God on this"?* Yes or no. If yes, then reflect is this about the gospel or about me? If it is the gospel, then ask yourself, *"Is my work being done in my strength or God's strength?"* If it's God's strength, then the critics have helped you reaffirm the vision God gave you! Once you've confirmed that this vision is from God, ask this question *"How do I protect the vision?"* Practice the vision validation like Nehemiah did. He didn't merely ignore his critics. He heard their words, tested them and used them to validate God's vision on his life.

Remember you are not a victim because you are criticized. Criticism can reaffirm the vision God has given you. The more progress you make on the vision the greater the attacks will be and the stronger your critics will want to destroy you.

The attacks came from my inner circle, as they usually do. Just like in the Garden of Eden; Satan who at the time was still not yet a fallen angel, still known as Lucifer. Just as my inner circle became jealous of me, Lucifer became jealous of Adam and Eve. Humans are made in the direct image of God, angels are not. We have something Satan will never have. He sat back and admired all the animals and creatures in the garden God had created. He strategically chose the serpent. The serpent was the most beautiful creature and highly intelligent. The serpent didn't deceive Eve overnight. Again, this was strategically planned out. The serpent befriended Eve. He had become a sort of confident she confided in. Eve grew to have quite a trust and friendship with the serpent. The enemy strategically plants people like the serpent in our lives during particular seasons. The season I recently came out of, there were multiple serpents planted by the enemy. His incessant goal is to take, steal, kill, and destroy. He manipulates circumstances, and inspires evil, disguising his activities behind the shroud of people or things. Many in my inner circle had betrayed me. They were people I trusted and called friends. It was just as Eve considered the serpent her friend, when in fact the enemy planted him there for her demise. The enemy knows that if he can keep us sick or out of church, he will keep us from accomplishing the ultimate plan and purpose God has for our lives. His goal is to destroy it any way possible, no matter what it takes.

Sometimes pain is a gift to help you understand what you need to change.

I have more awareness of others now, thanks to my husband. He usually sees things before I do. I tend to fight him on it and then I surrender. My husband recognized my former business partner as an opportunist long before I did. She was cunning and calculated. I imagine similar to the serpent who tricked Eve. Not letting the bad things that happen to you define you is essential to your growth. Choose to pick yourself up and keep going. You may not feel like it but push through and eventually the vivacious feelings towards life will return again. No one ever said owning your own business would be easy, only that it would be worth it.

One of the things I learned while processing this last season of my life is I don't have to be growing my business at massive speeds and levels every year. My growth in this season has been less about my business and more about myself. My dream was to have a real estate team selling massive volumes. God's plan was so much better. We have completely restructured our entire company. It looks nothing today like it did even just one short year ago. Getting on the same page with my husband has taken me time though completely rewarding. He has been with our business for one year now. During the last year he has worked diligently to cut our monthly budget. And within one year's time he cut it by fifty percent. All of this has allowed me to stress less, work less hours, and spend more time with my precious family. I have also come to acknowledge I need to listen to him. He usually catches or sees things before I do. I write him off too quickly and think he is just paranoid. God has placed him in my life to be a voice of reason. My husband truly wants the best for me and I trust him completely. I have learned listening to him first can protect me from problems and pain.

If you leave just one piece out of your life, you get a very different result.

The gift of enduring this past season of my life was finding true happiness from within, recognizing who my loyal friends are and seeing my husband as a leader. Someone I could trust and follow not only at home but also with our business. What a rewarding gift. For me, it's no longer about hitting massive numbers and taking home a six figure income. Nor is it about being number one or at the top! Don't buy into the meme that, *"bigger is better"*. Staying small may not be for everyone. For me I found excepting it difficult, but now I have actually come to love it. I couldn't be happier because each one of my steps has been established by God. Hard times and life wrecking your dreams can't always be avoidable. So when you find yourself moving through them remember resilience is about growth and a lesson learned. It's realizing you can recover from setbacks, wrecked dreams, adapt to the change and keep going in the face of adversity.

I can relate to this quote by Dylan Crain. *"So whenever your plans fall by the wayside remember that God is simply saving you."* Saving you for something unimaginably greater, not necessarily bigger but certainly greater. God might just wreck your dreams and that's the best possible thing that could happen, at least it was for me.

Strategies for Building Your Resilience

1. Are your friendships and relationships balanced with give and take? Your approach can either drive or hinder your success.

_____
_____
_____

2. Are you respecting the leaders and authorities God has placed in your life? God will sometimes intentionally place them there for your protection.

_____
_____
_____

3. What could God be saving you from? So your plans didn't work out. Your dreams were wrecked. Could it be he is saving you for something imaginably greater?

_____
_____
_____

About Betsy Ferguson

Betsy received her Bachelors of Science in Interior Design from Liberty University in 2008. With a declining job market and a pile of student loan debt she had to get creative. She landed a job with a local builder/developer. He quickly realized Betsy was highly driven and needed more financially. He encouraged her to obtain her Real Estate License. Betsy has now come full circle. Over two years ago she paid off her nearly $100,000 in student loan debt and today she owns and runs her real estate brokerage out of the building she worked in fresh out of college.

Betsy's warm and contagious personality is what sets her apart. Her greatest joy is her husband Matt and their beautiful, 3 year old daughter Layla Grayce. The Ferguson's absolutely love Lynchburg, Virginia! They have called Lynchburg home for over a decade. They have built 2 homes here. You will quickly see within her that family and people are what matter most. There is no denying Betsy's drive. Persistence and determination have embodied her core and launched Betsy forward into success.

With nearly eight years of experience in her local real estate market Betsy understands the importance of getting a home *"stage"* ready to sell while she strategically puts together a marketing package for success. Her clients enjoy her honest, down to earth approach and value her years of training and wisdom. Buyers appreciate her interior design expertise to see the potential of a new space. Betsy's years of background in New Construction sets her apart for those buyers looking to build or purchase a brand new home. Betsy has achieved to successfully navigate over 500 families on their journey they call home.

Contact Betsy
- Website: www.LynchburgsFinest.com
- Instagram: www.instagram.com/dear_betsy_
- Facebook: www.facebook.com/BetsyFergusonInc
- Email: Betsy@LynchburgsFinest.com

LIVING LIKE DREW
by Karen White

LIVING LIKE DREW

I will never forget the rainy day in June 2012 when my husband called me to tell me that the 26-year-old son of some dear friends and his wife had been in a car accident on Interstate 10. The tone of my husband's voice told me what I dreaded to ask; Drew was dead and his 7-month pregnant wife was in the hospital. Drew's wife and unborn baby girl were discharged the next day, with only a minor physical injury, to a life that would forever be changed.

The church ladies (of which I am proudly one) immediately sprang into action; what could we clean, cook, or do to help this family deal with an unthinkable, unimaginable loss. I have never met a person who knew anyone in this family who had anything negative to say about them…they are not the *"perfect"* family, but they are a family full of genuinely wonderful, loving people…and all of us who knew and loved them grieved deeply with them during this time.

It is easy to find examples of families who have suffered similar tragedies. It is far too common to lose children to car accidents, unexpected illnesses, violence, or other tragedies, but the story of the MacLean family is uncommon in how they dealt with their loss, and have turned it into a legacy that can only be described as miraculous. Their story helps me to re-define resilience.

Resilience is often defined as the ability to *"return to the ORIGINAL form, or position after being bent, pressed or stretched"* or *"to recovery readily from illness, depression, adversity, or the like."* Many people refer to *resilience"* as *"bouncing back"* from some difficulty. That is not the type of resilience that the MacLean family models for me, and everyone who encounters them, even to this day. Their form of resilience is so much more powerful than simply returning to the *"original form"* of their family, and it is based on something so fundamentally powerful as to be life-sustaining and life-altering. The type of resilience the MacLean family embodies is not simply *"getting through"* a tough situation, or *"getting over"* something difficult. It is fundamentally different than that.

This type of resilience shows up in the form of sustained, positive outcome, in the face of seemingly impossible circumstances.

The difference is grounded on the understanding that such resilience is not humanly possible, but it is possible for humans, if they choose to accept the power that comes from their Heavenly Father to make such outcome possible. It is not possible, in solely human strength, for a mother to bury her son, and believe that *"life still has promise."* It is not possible, in solely human strength, for a single mother to raise her daughter without her husband, soul mate and life partner, and believe that *"life still has possibility."* It is not possible, in solely human strength for a father or brother to look at common, everyday events without a son, or brother, and believe *"life still has the potential for happiness and fulfillment."* But, with the strength that comes from a firm belief in the power of a loving God and a faithful Savior, all of these are possible.

Where can this strength be found, and how can we be sure?

There are several factors that contribute to this type of resilience, and some key verses to illustrate the power that comes from a Heavenly Father who never wants to leave us in a dark place. This type of resilience comes to those who are *"strong in the Lord."*

"Be strong in the Lord and in his mighty power. Put on the full armor of God, so that you can take your stand against, the devil's schemes. For our struggle in not against flesh and blood, but against the rules, against the authorities, against the powers of this dark world, and against the spiritual forces of evil in the heavenly realms. Therefore put on the full armor of God, so that when the day of evil comes, you may be able to stand your ground, and after you have done everything, to stand. Stand firm then, with the belt of truth buckled around your waist, with the breastplate of righteousness in place, and with your feet fitted with the readiness that comes from the gospel of peace. In addition to all this, take up the shield of faith, with which you can extinguish all the flaming arrows of the evil one. Take the helmet of salvation and the sword of the Spirit, which is the word of God. And pray in the Spirit on all occasions with all kinds of prayers and requests."
- Ephesians 6:10-18.

This type of resilience is grounded on knowing who God is and that He is on your side. Joshua 1:9 reminds us that God has commanded us to *"be strong and courageous,"* and promises that *"the Lord your God will be with you wherever you go."* Certainly, this type of understanding allows us to walk through the most difficult situations, and not feel alone. There is more to resilience than not feeling alone, however. There is an attitude about the situation that is completely counter to what most of us feel when faced with devastating or difficult situations. Resilient people, like the MacLeans, are thankful people. I don't mean to suggest that they are thankful that they lost their son, brother, or husband, but they are people who have a genuinely grateful outlook on life. James 1:2-4 tells us to *"consider it pure joy when we face trials of many kinds."* This verse used to confuse me. I had a difficult time understanding what it meant, and how it could be possible to consider a trial *"joy"*. I learned a valuable lesson as I watched the MacLean family navigate the weeks and months following Drew's death. What I say was there can be joy amidst sadness.

Joy is not the same as "happiness"...it is a level of understanding of God's love and peace that surpasses any fleeting feeling or emotion.

The peace of God that transcends our understanding brings this kind of joy, and that peace and that joy sustain you through the trials, so that you emerge from them changed in a way that only God can do. I will never forget a Facebook post that Drew's wife Allison posted before the birth of their daughter, where she had a painting of her favorite verse, John 16:33. That verse says, *"In this world you will have trouble. But take heart, I have overcome the world."* For me, that post, and that picture will forever be ingrained in my memory as an example of the kind of resilience I hope to grow in my own life. A faith that would sustain a young mother through a life event she surely didn't expect. And although she never expected it, she was prepared for it, through her faith and trust in her Savior.

Another truth about resilience is that it is a matter of focus...

When we find ourselves in a disappointing, difficult, or disheartening situation we have a choice. We can focus on our trouble, or we can focus on our Savior. It is impossible to focus on both, and where you focus goes, your energy flows. What I learned from the MacLean family was the incredible power of focus. Psalm 62:8 reminds me to trust in Him at all times and to pour out my heart to Him, for God *"is your refuge."* 1 Peter 5:7 reminds me that I can *"cast all my anxiety on Him, because He cares for me"*, and Hebrews 12 promises that if I *"run with perseverance the race marked out"* for me, I will not grow weary or lose heart. This is the promise of focus...the foundation of the kind of resilience that allows a family to go through a tragedy and emerge changed, but in a positive way.

How did the MacLean family emerge from their tragedy changed? In response to their loss of a beloved son, brother, and husband, they started a foundation to encourage others to live like Drew; focusing on the character traits of generosity, strong faith, compassion, and love, not just in words but in action! Within one year of Drew's accident and death, the 'Live Like Drew Foundation' had spearheaded. The first annual Live Like Drew day, where community members were challenged to *"live like Drew"*…by performing random acts of kindness, spreading Christ's love, and then sharing about their experience on social media, all in Drew's honor and memory. The 'Live Like Drew Foundation' (www.LiveLikeDrew.com) established a scholarship for local high school students, which is funded by an annual softball tournament, capturing Drew's love of the sport and of local students. All of these events bring positivity and love and compassion to the community, and they were all started to honor a man who lived out those qualities quietly and profoundly in his 26 years. His legacy lives on, multiplied by the many people who have come to know about Drew and what he stood for. This is the model of what resiliency can do…not a return to the original, but a positive outcome.

Do the MacLeans (and all of Drew's many friends) miss Drew? Undoubtedly so. Would they all love to have him here present with them? Most assuredly, yes. Does the loss of Drew define this family? Absolutely not. They have turned tragedy into triumph and they have changed their community, and made an eternal impact. And that is far better than simply *"bouncing back."*

So, what can we learn from the MacLeans to apply to our lives? I pray that we never find ourselves mourning the loss of a child, or facing some other tragedy, but what I know is that we will face difficult situations of a much less tragic scale throughout our lives. If we can apply the principles of resilient living, then none of those difficulties needs to derail us from enjoying a full, rich life. There are 5 lessons that I learned from the MacLeans that I believe can be applied to any difficulty that we encounter in our lives, whether that's the disappointing loss of a job or career, an unexpected diagnosis, the end of a long-term relationship, or the regular disappointments that befall us as we live in this fallen world.

The <u>first lesson</u> undergirds the other four, and that is TAKE YOUR THOUGHTS CAPTIVE.

This is biblical advice that we find in 2 Corinthians 10:5 *"Wedemolish arguments and every pretension that sets itself up againstthe knowledge of Christ, and we take captive every thought to make it obedient to Christ."* It is certainly easy and understandable to find ourselves with negative thoughts when we encounter difficult situations. It is easy and understandable to find ourselves asking *"why me"* or *"why not me"* or *"why did this happen (or not happen)"* in the wake of a disappointing or difficult situation. We can easily fall into the trap that it is impossible that we will emerge from the difficulty in any form that would be recognized as *"better,"* which is, as we remember, the goal of living a resilient life. Instead, if we can recognize the thoughts that would have us question God's plan or His intention toward us, and take those thoughts captive, we are making a huge step toward resilience, and away from the temptation of the *"pity party."* Once we have captured our thoughts, how can we make those thoughts obedient to Christ? Philippians 4:8 gives us guidance: *"Whatever is true, whatever is noble, whatever is right, whatever is pure, whatever is lovely, whatever is admirable–if anything is excellent or praiseworthy– think about such things."*

If we follow this guidance, *"the God of peace will be with"* us, and we have the ability to emerge from difficult situations without the baggage of negativity that will taint our present and our future.

Once we have taken our thoughts captive, we can move to the <u>second lesson</u> - HELP SOMEONE ELSE.

When we find ourselves in a difficult or trying situation, it is tempting to retreat into our own troubles…but that is a recipe for getting stuck! Instead, change your perspective and help someone else. I have a favorite saying by an unknown author that really speaks to how serving someone else can actually help us become more resilient: *"The strongest people make time to help others, even if they're struggling with their own personal demons."* I can think of many people in my own life who have been in difficult situations, yet have found the time to do something for someone else. In all of those situations, I find inspiration in their *"strength"*, and their actions remind me that it is difficult to focus on my own hurt and disappointment while I am focused on helping someone else. Robert Ingersoll said *"we rise by lifting others,"* and I would argue that quote nicely captures one of the ways that we can become resilient in our lives…by changing our focus or perspective. The late Dr. Wayne Dyer is known for reminding us that *"If you change the way you look at things, the things you look at change."*

Changing our perspective allows us to live resilient lives.

The <u>third lesson</u> on resilience I learned from my friends was to GIVE IT TO GOD - REALLY GIVE IT TO HIM.

I find in my own life that when I am faced with a big difficulty, like a colon cancer diagnosis at age 40, it is easy to understand that the outcome of the surgery is completely out of my control, and therefore, it is easier to turn that over to the care and control of my Heavenly Father. What isn't as easy is turning over those *"lesser"* difficulties. In the *"non-life threatening"* situations, I struggle with hanging on to *"responsibility"* for those situations. (I have often joked that I am a *"responsibility addict"*, and it is true, I use being responsible as a way to maintain *"control"* of a situation). Surrender is a simple concept - we've all heard someone say *"Let go and Let God"* - but not always easy to do in practice. I read a quote by an evangelist named Winkie Pratney that really struck me. Winkie notes that *"God does not guide those who want to run their own life."* If we really want to live a resilient life, we need to fully admit that we are powerless to control the situations around us…as much as we might want to believe we are in *"control"*…we aren't, and continuing to hang on to situations and attempt to orchestrate the solution limits the solution to what we can conceive and create; which is nowhere near what God can do with a situation. I am convinced that the 'Live Like Drew Foundation', and *"Live Like Drew"* day are both products of the MacLean's willingness to surrender the situation to God, and to follow where He lead. John 14:27 promises God's peace to us, and reminds us to *"not let your hearts be troubled and do not be afraid."*

The <u>fourth lesson</u> to living a resilient life is to UNDERSTAND - NO EMBRACE - THE REALITY THAT WE MAY NOT SEE OR UNDERSTAND GOD'S PLAN.

This lesson I learned was a bit more difficult to fully grasp, but I have witnessed the power of this lesson in the time since Drew's passing. I remember several occasions when I would see Drew's family at church, and especially at the first annual The Drew softball tournament. I would question how and why the situation could be God's plan. I crave understanding of God's plans for my life, and that is especially true when I find myself facing a situation that wasn't in MY plan. When I have faced disappointing business endeavors or hosted workshops where nobody registered or worse, people registered, and then never paid or showed up, I have questioned whether I was on the right track or whether what was happening was part of God's plan for my life. In some situations I have had the blessing to recognize how God's plan actually benefitted me, but in others, I have not received any *"explanation"* from God as to what His plan is and how it is unfolding. It is tempting to wait for complete understanding before we move in life, and it is especially tempting to do so in the face of great uncertainty or difficulty or disappointment, but I believe one of the traits of a resilient person is the acceptance that God doesn't owe me an explanation and the understanding that I may never understand why something happened a certain way or didn't happen the way I wanted it to play out. In order to live this type of resilient life, it is imperative to know who God is, and fully "understand and embrace His promises. That information allows us to trust God, and His plan, even when (especially when) we don't understand it. I have often heard people say, *"God doesn't waste a hurt,"* and although I do not believe God causes hurt, I believe this statement to be true, because I believe what Scripture says about God's character, His love for us, and the fact that He works out a plan for our good.

The <u>fifth and final lesson</u> I've learned about living a resilient life is YOU MAY NEVER BE READY FOR A TRAGEDY OR DIFFICULTY, BUT YOU CAN BE PREPARED.

I don't consider this tricky word play, I think there's a differencein this context between being *"ready"* and being *"prepared."* What I mean is that no mentally healthy person would ever invite a tragedy or difficulty into their lives, but they can be prepared once that difficulty comes. I have a dear friend who often reminds our Sunday school class that when we're faced with difficulty we can get *"better"* or we can get *"bitter."* Those words of wisdom have found a place in my heart and mind, and I know they were some of the words of wisdom that the MacLean family relied on as they traveled a road they certainly weren't *"ready"* to travel. Resilient people are *"prepared"* in the sense that they have built a strong foundation of such wisdom. They aren't searching for some wisdom at the time of the difficulty or tragedy; they can draw it up from its storage location and put it into immediate action when it's needed. In fact, resilient people don't even have to search long for such wisdom to surface, because it is a part of who they are. Immersing ourselves in the truths and wisdom of other resilient people, and God's word helps to build that strong foundation to prepare us for what lies ahead.

We are often surprised when we're faced with difficulty, but we shouldn't be. Jesus didn't promise us a life of easy sailing, or a trouble free existence. He promised just the opposite: *"In this world you will have trouble. But take heart! I have overcome the world."* - John 16:33. I think this verse sums up resilient living perfectly…there WILL be trouble…but TAKE HEART! JESUS HAS OVERCOME THE WORLD (trouble)!

Strategies for Building Your Resilience

1. Take your thoughts captive!

What are some thoughts in your head that you find is an obstacle for something in your life right now?

_____
_____
_____

2. Help someone else.

The opportunity is in front of you right now. Who could you help so that it shifts your focus to serve which in turn will help you change your thought patterns?

_____
_____
_____

3. Give it to God.

What is something that you need to give to God so he can carry it for you?

_____
_____
_____

4. Understand that we may never see or understand God's plan. We can however decide to be prepared.

What are some things you can do to help you be prepared for when setbacks come your way? What specific actions could you take? Who could you spend time with?

_____
_____
_____

5. We will face difficulty, but we are equipped for resiliency - not to *"bounce back"* but to *"survive and thrive."* Imagine feeling that you are thriving even in the midst of uncertainty. How could that change your life and your relationships?

_____
_____
_____

About Karen White

Karen White is a John Maxwell Certified Coach, Teacher, and Speaker. As a *"DREAM Locksmith"* she helps people discover or rediscover their God-given dream, and become their *"best self."*

Helping others discover their gifts and talents and create a life where people life into their purpose is Karen's passion! Holocaust survivor Elie Wiesel once noted that at the end of our lives we won't be asked why we didn't accomplish certain things, but we will have to answer the question: *"Why didn't you become you? Why didn't you become all that you are?"* Karen wants to help others respond to that question with a resounding, *"I DID!"*

Karen has served with the US Air Force as both an active duty officer and civil service attorney for nearly 30 years. She began writing in 2015 because she aims to live by George Eliot's quote, *"It's never too late to be what you might have been!"*

To reach Karen visit her on the web at www.JohnMaxwellGroup.com/KarenWhite.

Contact Karen
- Website: www.JohnMaxwellGroup.com/KarenWhite
- Email: KarenWhite717@gmail.com
- Phone: 850-276-4504

LIFE IS A JOURNEY OF RETAKES
by Gary King

LIFE IS A JOURNEY OF RETAKES

Life brings us challenges that range from emotional, financial and physical to the unthinkable, and potentially unresolvable. Many suffer from what can be commonly known as PTSD (post-traumatic stress disorder). The average person in many cases lacks the emotional tools and references to become what is considered resilient, or responsible, which simply means able to respond to life's challenging situations in a positive way.

We are brought into this life without an owners' manual, unlike almost everything in the material world. In most cases, by the time we are five years old, we have been mentally and emotionally programmed to respond based on information that resides in our subconscious mind. Our subconscious mind does not have the ability to reason. It is just a storage facility of the brain much like a computer hard drive. In many cases, this storage facility works directly against our quality of life, and our physical health based on what is programmed before we have developed called *"cognitive skills."* These are the skills that start at about six to eight years old when we have developed the power of reason. The average person may go through their entirelifetime never realizing that 90% of their life is controlled by the subconscious mind, and only 10% is controlled by the conscious mind. Simply put, you have 10% free will in your daily choices.

At an early age, we learn to objectify people; objects to fill emotional voids that either bring on pleasure or pain. We start by venturing out and away from the objects to see how far we can get before we need the emotional void once again filled by an object; be it a parent, stuffed animal, food, or nurturing. This is generally the beginning of a life-long unconscious pattern which has everything to with the human ability be resilient and rebound from life's small and overwhelming challenges.

Consider the idea of driving a car while looking in the rear-view mirror. If the car moves forward without you looking where you are going, the obvious result is a crisis.

Now come to the reality that many humans are doing the exact same thing. They are looking back while trying to rebound from life's sometimes predictable and many times unpredictable consequences. We get programmed to auto respond to unpleasant, unhealthy, and horrific situations as a reaction rather than an action.

Peoples' lives become giant chess boards which involve moving objects to get emotional results when in reality we are attempting to exert control over what we actually have zero control over. Without a basic emotional owner's manual, it is not difficult to venture down the path of learned helplessness and learned hopelessness. When that happens, we seriously limit our rebound options. Then add to the human enigma the attachment factor, the driving force that keeps us emotionally bound to that which we think we cannot live without, be it a person, place, or thing. Without healthy emotionally resources, we flounder like ships without rudders, going where ever the emotional tide takes us, or sinking like the Titanic.

What then is the secret to resilience?

You must fully understand the why behind un-resourceful emotions. Once you comprehend that human behavior is learned, you then can start a process of un-learning. Why do we attach ourselves to the inevitable loss? When you unlearn that lesson, you learn that the only thing you can ever really own is YOU.

You can own your full potential, or live in denial. You can take full responsibility for your life, and give up the blame game. You can stop managing the effects of your life, and start managing the cause.

Managing effects looks like this: *"I need to earn love; I need to be a pleaser; I need to say yes, when I really mean No; I need to be emotionally unavailable to protect myself; I need to hide my true feelings to be accepted; I need to constantly compare myself to others."* These are also examples of low self-worth.

The foundation of resilience is connected directly to self-worth.

If you manage the 'cause,' you are managing your original life lesson as a child and indicating that the original cause is you simply did not grow up with healthy self-worth (or low self-worth.) That is original cause at the foundation level. All that transpires afterward is managing the effects.

Imagine living your life without the fear of mistakes. Is there really such a thing as a *"miss-take?"* We tend to stack our perceived mistakes one after another which ultimately makes us emotionally bound and unworthy of resilience. In the movie industry, there is no such thing as a mistake. While filming a movie, they are called *"re-takes."* In life, if we treated what we call mistakes as re-takes for the purpose of learning and attaining wisdom, rather than so much emphasis put on levels of intelligence, we would develop the emotional wisdom to support resilience.

As an example, we have been taught primary lessons like, *"It is better to give than receive."* However, our subconscious mind interprets that to mean, *"Giving is good, and receiving is not good".*

If our primary lesson was, *"It is better to give AND receive"* our lives would completely shift. Our ability would be *"response-able"* and resilient to all of life's challenges.

Life is not an "End Game"; It is a journey of re-takes.

Happiness and a life well lived is not the same as short-term pleasure. Happiness starts on the path of wisdom which requires looking forward and moving forward. The real 'you' accepts the past and creates your desired future and quality of life, and 'Pays Life Forward' for everyone.

About Gary King

Gary King is a speaker, author, and successful entrepreneur. His back ground is diverse and exhilarating. Over the last 15 years at global events, Gary passionately developed a profound message and travels globally 6 months each year to share his message with leaders and entrepreneurs, in schools, prisons, and to teen groups. His message is timely and riveting on the subject of Character, Ethics, Integrity, and Forgiveness. His message has appeared in articles in Oprah Magazine, O's Guide to Life, Positive Impact magazine and has had numerous articles published related to, 'Character is our Bailout.'

Gary's life story is filled with amazing accomplishments and honors, and many unthinkable nightmares, yet he ventures forward with a heart and soul of a victor.

Gary's messages, branded and trademarked as *"The Power of Truth"* and, *"The Happiness Formula"* and *"The Ultimate Life Makeover"*, has dramatically enhanced the lives of thousands of people in many cultures.

Gary is passionate about bringing the United States and theWorld, back to a foundation of Self Worth, Character, and Integrity starting with the public schools, and helping returning veterans rise above the overwhelming challenges of PTSD. He has also created a non-profit foundation to serve those that are without resources and in need of emotional support.

Gary's most recent book, *The Happiness Formula®: The Ultimate Life Makeover* ™ has been recently been adapted for a movie.

Visit www.GaryKingLive.com to take the 21 Day Self Worth Challenge, The 24 Hour Truth Challenge, and The 24 Hour Forgiveness Challenge.

Contact Gary
- Website: www.GaryKingLive.com

LAYERS OF LIFE
by Tricia Andreassen

LAYERS OF LIFE

"There are always hidden layers within the landscape of resilience."
– Tricia Andreassen

Just prior to the final edits of this book my husband and I went to the smoky mountains in Western North Carolina and Eastern Tennessee for our wedding anniversary. Every day there seemed to be a chance of rain in the afternoon and sure enough, as the weatherman predicted we did experience storms rolling through.

Here is what I found in observing the change in weather patterns dancing across the sky and melding with the mountain edges. When the clouds swooped in from above mixing with the curves and ridges of the mountains, the most beautiful views emerged. What a dichotomy to life isn't it?

For if it were clear and sunny all the time we would become bored after a while seeing the same view over and over again. In the valleys I watched the clouds dip into the crevices between the mountains, the view changed to something I could not take my eyes off of. Driving up Roan Mountain at just over 6,000 feet it was clear on the road and to the right you could see clearly for miles. The clouds mixing into the tops of the mountains and moving at a rapid pace gave such a dramatic scene you could hardly take your eyes off the shadows that were casting upon the greens. To the left you could hear remnants of thunder and see the mist of the cloud moving rapidly across the road, blanketing the view around us. Sure enough, as we made it to the top of the mountain we could hardly see our hand in front of us. The mountain midst had enveloped us where it was going to be a bit unsettling to drive out of those conditions. It gave me pause. It provided a unique perspective.

It is in our nature that although we like the certainty of things, we also crave change or variety. Of course, the double edge sword of the uncertainty can be like the weather. Sometimes interesting, bringing a unique view to an opportunity, and sometimes an all-out scary view where we have no idea what the road ahead looks like. We have all known those moments. I am in one of those right now as of this particular chapter. My 15 year old recently had shoulder surgery and it is the second time in 2 weeks we have driven from North Carolina to Michigan to deal with a sudden diagnoses of AML (Acute Myeloid Leukemia) in the family (see my following chapter in regards to this). With that said, there are many layers in life that bring vast changes in our conditions.

<u>We have layers of our personality</u> – complex as we are and even after many years of research the human brain much less the depth of creativity and understanding has not been fully unlocked. The mystery is there for us to explore the possibilities.

<u>We have layers of relationships</u> – some of the people in our life are simple and easy without much depth while others are rich, deep, and sometimes complicated. One of my close friends, Dara, shared with me a few years ago that has always resonated. She said, *"Tricia, some people are to come into your life for a short period of time and some for a long time. Regardless of the time, it is meant to be as God has plans for us to learn and perhaps be in that person's life for that time to learn something."* I have to say her loving and flexible comment about relationships is one of the most beautiful moments I have experienced. In the 11 years I have known her I have never heard a harsh word out of her. She has lost friends and she has gained friends and even in those changing patterns she chooses an outlook of understanding. Very much like a meteorologist who looks at the weather and recognizes the changes for what they are (while intrigued at those patterns), she has learned to

be flexible to what those relationships may bring. Being 10 years younger than me she has been a phenomenal teacher in my life still today.

<u>We have layers within ourselves</u> – I imagine that all of us have said something at some particular point of, *"I just don't know if I can make it through this."* Perhaps it was a death of someone close to you. Perhaps it was something like a divorce where you were shaken from every bit of your core. Maybe a scenario was like a thunderstorm with a flash flood where you had several things happen at the same time and you couldn't gain your footing to save your life. Yet…Somehow you weathered through. In the midst of the storm you were in the throes of survival. And while in that, something was exposed within you that gave you the ability to hold on for the ride; to fight your way back; to hold on that this would pass and you would survive. That is why living our life reminds me of a tree growing; specifically an olive tree. You see, an Olive tree can thrive in rough terrain. It thrives with little water and in desert conditions apt to wind and rain. Yet, it is known for its resilience to the threat of fire. In its growth and resolve it takes on some of the most beautiful trunk structures that show strength and yet beauty at the same time.

And that is not the only tree that is resilient. The palm tree lives in the most diverse areas of winds and storms and yet it does not seem to yield to those storms. Instead, it blows and it bends. Sometimes it looks like there is no way it is going to live as the leaves and fruit come crashing to the ground. But guess what? It is the storms that create the strength of the tree! It is after the storm that the trunk becomes STRONGER. It is after the effects of the weathers conditions that the trunk bends to form a beautiful shape along the waters' edge. Just close your eyes and think about it for a minute. When you think of a beautiful palm tree on this island next to the water I bet it has some type of unique bend to it.

Perhaps that is why God created such layers in all things in life. Now, don't get me wrong I am not saying that God brings those challenges necessarily. We must remember that he doesn't control our free will. I sincerely believe that he also doesn't sit up there on a throne and say *"I want to give a problem to Tricia today."* For I know the miraculous experiences that he provides me in the storms of what has been thrown to me. Unfortunately, we must realize that as God cast out evil in heaven that evil manifests into different scenarios of dis-ease, depression, illness, conflict, and so much more. However what I have found is it in in the layers of the challenge or uncertainty is when the GIFT comes; the other part of the weather that brings something beautiful to the overall picture.

As I reflect on the drive in the mountains, admiring the landscape and the trees reactions to the weather, I am reminded that it is in the cycle of life that builds our resolve and our resilience. For it is in those moments that the most beautiful blossoms emerge off those leaves. The rain creates a waterfall of beauty that would not have existed. The grass would not come back greener. The butterflies would not pond. The deer would not venture out with their young.

There would be no life. There would be no resilience to come back even stronger than before. This is why I have a meaning for each letter in the word LIFE. It creates awareness and mindfulness on how to build resilience:

LOVE - Love is talked about and it is a word used so often and yet the profound impact of love on resilience is remarkable. To be able to bounce back from the challenges life throws at us we must be able to:

Love in the possibility of what lies before us, even though we may not be able to see it. Call it hope. Call it love. To me, when things have been difficult I have been able to look at those in my life who I love and who count on me. It is in that love that responsibility and perseverance arises. The love for them I have is so strong that I must be willing to stay the course even when it seems impassible.

Love for myself, even though I am in the middle fo beating myself up at the moment, the love I have for my life is stronger than the problem in front of me. The belief in me is an ingredient of love within myself. Sure I may struggle in loving some parts of me (my weight is one), but overall I love my spirit and my heart that God has given me. It is in that place that I become resilient.

1. How could you bring the feeling of self-love into your life more on a continual basis?

_____
_____
_____

2. What would be some ways that you could show love to others?

_____
_____
_____

3. Exercise: Pretend that you are in high school or college. Imagine the perspective of the person that would have the crush on you. Write from their standpoint of why they admire you and love you so much. Yes. Write yourself a love letter. Give it to a friend or family member and have them mail it to you in six months. You will be amazed it will come at the more opportune time.

_____
_____
_____

INSPIRATION - When a situation looks bleak and we feel like we don't have the energy to move forward, getting inspired about something, anything, can help make it through. Perhaps you may not know it is inspiration that is happening at the moment. It could come in the humming of a song that resonates with how you are feeling. It may come in the form of writing a poem, painting a picture, or even cooking a meal for someone. I have seen it manifest through people who they are going through their own personal storm and even still they find ways to volunteer to help others in need. These are the sparks of inspiration that allow us to grab hold of optimistic viewpoints and of better moments ahead. Inspiration can create feelings of gratitude, of hope, and of contribution which all build resilience.

1. When the last time you did an activity that was considered a hobby?

_____
_____
_____

2. What did you love about doing it? How did you feel when you were in the process of it?

_____
_____
_____

3. Exercise: Think back to when you were a child. What was some of the things that you did as activities that were fun for you? For me, I realized it was singing and putting on shows in my neighborhood. In fourth grade, I wrote my own book of poems. I loved to color and paint things. It was only in this reflection that I realized these were things that grounded me as an adult too.

Write and reflect about those moments that brought you joy. What have you realized about yourself from this exercise?

_____
_____
_____

FAITH - You read so much about faith in these stories. It is a core element of resilience and yet many times faith is so hard to describe. Often misconstrued as a religious word it is so much more profound. Faith is believing in something that even when the odds are stacked against you, you lean in to the knowing that all will be okay. It is a blind element that hangs in the air mixed with emotion, hope, and intuition.

1. How do you get faith?

_____
_____
_____

2. If this is something you struggle with, what are some things you could do that could help you build your faith? Why would that be helpful for you in your life?

_____
_____
_____

3. If you had more faith in your life, what could that do to your personal relationships?

_____
_____
_____

Your work?

_____
_____
_____

Your dreams?

_____
_____
_____

ENERGY - This is a word that isn't discussed much it seems yet it is a catalyst in every single activity in our existence. Our actions create energy. Our environment and the people we associate with create energy. We have all experience moments where we have been around certain situations where we have said *"I just didn't have a good vibe"* or perhaps you said *"That person seems to always bring me down."* It is important to remember these things when it comes to building one's resilience.

Environment contributes greatly to your mindset and the energy that feeds not only your logical mind but your spirit and soul. According to physics, energy can neither be created nor destroyed; rather, it transforms from one form to another. When you are around those who focus on negative things that will naturally transfer to you. It is a universal law of energy.

1. Who is in your life right now that brings positive energy to you in good times and bad?

_____
_____
_____

2. Who could be contributing to stress in your life right now due to their transference of energy to you?

_____
_____
_____

3. What could you do to improve the energy around you so your mindset is resilient?

_____
_____
_____

4. Exercise: Go somewhere in nature that allows you to meditate and find stillness in the environment around you. What do you realize about your breathing? How does your spirit feel? What could you do to shift your energy to a state that lifts you in times of challenge?

_____
_____
_____

THE REFLECTION OF RESILIENCE
by Tricia Andreassen

THE REFLECTION OF RESILIENCE

How interesting to be sitting in the same chair here in Michigan at my Mother and Father in Laws house where the meaning of resilience was brought to me so strongly to me months before.

While driving up from North Carolina to come see my dear Father-In-Law, who was diagnosed with Leukemia in the final edits of this book, my husband and I happen to see a massive storm in the distance blanketing the rolling hills of the Ohio plain. As we continued to drive the winds got stronger and the rains began to downpour causing it difficult to see the road ahead. But guess what? In the passenger seat I turned to my right to look out the window and when I did I saw the most incredible rainbow. I could see both the beginning of the rays stretching upward to the sky. What was unique was seeing the end of that arch meeting the ground on the other side. Yet, in the most top of the arch where the dark gray clouds lay, those rays couldn't be seen. Yet, they peeked through the other side to meet the ground on the other side.

It causes me to pause in the early morning hours and seeing the family pictures set in a wooden frame that looks like a tree. It reminds me that we do not know Life's twist and turns. As the branches on the tree, some of the branches are smooth while some have rough edges and knots in the bark.

While the candles of light burn beside me and I sit in this chair, I look to the wall and see a blanket collage of my husband's loving family; and my family that I am so blessed to be a part of. The collage shows glimpses into the 62 years that mom and dad have been through together and the creation of the family that continues to grow. In those pictures we see the smiling pictures, the hugs, and the different moments of life. What we don't see is all the intricate details that created the tapestry of it all. I can tell you what I do see. I see strength. I see resolve. I see perseverance and I see the gifts of RESILIENCE. Yes, resilience. It is always evolving, and leaving its remnants within the soil long after we may even know.

AFTER THE STORM - FINDING YOUR WAY BACK

by Tricia Andreassen

AFTER THE STORM - FINDING YOUR WAY BACK

I am so grateful for the tools of resilience for in the beginning of this book. I shared what I knew to be difficult times yet when looking back on this now in the final stages of this book I realize that we may never know what lies ahead and when resilience will need to rise up to meet us.

Isn't that how resilience is? It is needed in every moment of our life. At the middle stages of this book project I wrote about the season that I could reflect on and little did I know what would come in the final days of editing of this book.

On August 31, 2016 my dear father-in-law passed away, at home with his family by his side. From diagnosis to his last breath was a little over two weeks. Needless to say, we were in complete shock as this was a man who had come through all the difficulties of multiple heart attacks, surgeries, and valve replacements and somehow was always able to bounce back from many times being on the brink of death.

I have always said that there are two parallel paths that run at the same time, and I definitely experienced it in this situation. One path during these days showed the most beautiful experience I will always remember. We lifted one another in love, in physical touch, in sharing, in the care giving, and the home responsibilities. Since I am an early riser to the tune of 4 am most days to write, I had the unique gift to sit with Dad, hold his hand, sing to him, read, and tell him stories. In those quiet moments, I focused on pouring all my love and energy that I could into him while also taking time to meditate and pray deeply for our family.

The other side of the path was very dark at times: Learning

how hospice worked in a home setting, learning terms such as 'terminal restlessness' where Dad could not get comfortable and would be in pain. It was breaking our hearts in these moments not knowing what to do.

That is when God reminded me of the spiritual gifts he had given me. Through my fasting, prayer, reading, and meditation, I heard God talk to me about anointing and laying my hands on Dad to help ease his pain. This was something that had come to me, back in the beginning of 2015, with an angelic and Holy Spirit experience. I will save for another book, but I had not fully embraced it. Many times in prayer God would talk to me. Now looking back there are pages and pages of those words where God was calling me into the ministry to help in the healing of the heart, soul, and spirit.

It was only until my love for Dad became stronger than my discouraging voice, that I let God take over. As I focused on the spiritual gifts mentioned in Timothy, I allowed God to show his love THROUGH me. When I would rub my hands together, get them hot and place them on Dad's painful back his spirit would calm. Even my mother-in-law said, *"You have the touch"* but I knew it was the work of God's hand on this chapter in my life.

I share this with you because I want to encourage you to look at the two parallels that may run at the same time; like opposite sides of the coin. I don't know why this is, but it is a reminder for us to be aware of it. I also share this with you because as a researcher and teacher on resilience, I was able to take away something from this difficult time that I might not have shared with you.

Many stories have talked about how to manage in the storm and how to get through the storm. But now, in living this most recent experience I want to share with you how to become STRONGER AFTER THE STORM. You see, in the middle of the storm with Dad, many of us were on automatic pilot. Helping one another and care where needed while running errands and talking to the Doctors. I guess realizing it now, I was allowing God to use me to minister, comfort, pray, and do spiritual work, so I didn't have time to focus on what things would feel like afterward. I imagine that is true for most of us.

It was after Dad passed away that my body and spirit were showing signs of wear. But I was doing what I could to stand strong for my husband, son, and family. Then, in the car traveling back from Michigan the extreme exhaustion hit. It wasn't just an exhaustion of sleep. It was a combination of spiritual depletion. I don't ever remember experiencing before in my life.

Over the days of healing to replenish my mind, spirit, soul, and body I wrote those things that helped me refill my soul and focus on the beautiful experiences that can come out of loss and hardship. Isaiah 40:31 says, *"But those who hope in the LORD will renew their strength. They will soar on wings like eagles; they will run and not grow weary, they will walk and not be faint."* With those words, I stayed focused on knowing that God has me and has my purpose in his hands.

Here are recommendations for being stronger after the storm has passed:

1. Get outside even when it is hard to do at first.

You may not feel up to being around people or even talking to others on the phone. A simple walk around your yard can bring oxygen and healing into your body. Is there a favorite place for you go that is outside to help you reconnect with nature?

_____
_____
_____

2. Sleep. Listen to your body.

It's OKAY to sleep if you need to. People close to you may think that it is abnormal or that your naps are too long. Frompersonal experience this may be one of the best ways to let your whole self-rejuvenate, especially in the beginning. You will know if you are sleeping as an escape or if it is for self-healing. Stay connected and real with yourself during this process and honor what your body may be saying to you.

3. Find quiet. Dial into your intuition.

Those around you can give advice or want to keep you busy with ideas and plans. Know that the answer lies within you to serve what you need to heal fully. Don't be afraid that you might hurt others feelings. This time is about you and focusing on what your heart is calling you to do for healing.

4. Find ways to process.

Journal. Paint. Craft. Read. Meditate. Listen to music. Sing. Pray. Read your Bible. All of these help soothe the soul and process the healing that is needed to gain insight and help you move forward.

5. Release and Surrender.

For me knowing that Christ went through such pain to give me everlasting life allows me to look to his words for giving it to God. We have to remember that there are just some things out of our control but if we lean in to God's words and trust in the process, I promise he will see you through.

"When you pass through the waters, I will be with you; and when you pass through the rivers, they will not sweep over you. When you walk through the fire, you will not be burned; the flames will not set you ablaze." - Isaiah 43:2

Remember this...

The truth is that you will look back at the storm you have come from and realize the beautiful growth that has been provided. It is in this knowing that I am more trusting in the process because God has always carried me through. The gift in this has been the understanding of what Jesus and the disciples went through carrying the word of God throughout the land and often being criticized by those who were supposed to be of like mind and faith. It is in the knowing that others do not have your calling. They do not have your vision. They do not see what God sees in you. They do not understand what God is doing THROUGH you!

www.ingramcontent.com/pod-product-compliance
Lightning Source LLC
Chambersburg PA
CBHW071614080526
44588CB00010B/1125